THE SOFTBALL HANDBOOK

Susan Craig
Ken Johnson

LEISURE PRESS
Champaign, Illinois

Published by Leisure Press
A division of Human Kinetics Publishers, Inc.
Box 5076, Champaign, IL 61825-5076
1-800-342-5457
1-800-334-3665 (in Illinois)

Book design and production: Dee Elling
Photos on pages 6, 16, 20, 34, 40, 58, 88, 104, 109, 112, 120, 128, 130,
134, 148 and 160: Dave Benyak

Library of Congress Cataloging in Publication Data

Craig, Susan (Susan B.)
  The softball handbook.

  1. Softball—Coaching.   I. Johnson, Ken, 1944-
II. Title.
GV881.4.C6C7   1984   796.357'8   84-12253
ISBN 0-88011-260-3

Dedication

Special thanks to the members of the Lobo softball team—past and present—family and friends and associates whose talent, ideas and support made this book possible.

There were smiles and frowns
for the ups and downs
of those who believed and cared
who played with heart
and became a part
of the cherry and silver New Mexico dream.

Preface

The Softball Handbook was written in response to many requests for a fastpitch softball fundamentals book. It reflects the Lobo System designed by Susan Craig and Ken Johnson, coaches at the University of New Mexico in Albuquerque, N. M. The Lobo System is a teaching program based on the philosophy that fundamentals should be broken down into several parts, designed to develop the natural athlete through a step-by-step learning progression into a refined, highly skilled performer. All the drills are described as if the player is right-handed.

This text is not meant to be the last word in coaching softball. It depicts the fundamentals and philosophy of two highly successful coaches who loved to play softball and continue to be students of the game. Sharing knowledge and learning—two vital ingredients—is necessary for the growth of women's fastpitch softball. It is not necessary for all coaches to agree, but it is important for everyone to continue to analyze and understand in order to keep softball America's number-one sport.

Contents

1

Practice Organization

One of the keys to a successful program is practice organization. A coach must be both knowledgeable and able to teach that knowledge effectively. A team's performance is a reflection of what it has been taught, not what it has been told. Hours of preparation, determining how best to correlate information with the available talent and a coaching philosophy, must take place long before practice ever begins.

A well-thought-out plan of action must be developed to achieve success. First, develop a philosophy. Second, evaluate the players and determine the team's assets and liabilities. Third, make a checklist of what needs to be covered. Your philosophy will dictate which areas receive the highest priority. The team evaluation will indicate how best to use the ability available. The amount of time available will provide the guidelines in which the information must be covered. Practice prior to competition will differ from practice during the competitive season.

Draw a calendar for the total amount of time available, (e.g. six weeks). Assuming that by the first game the maximum amount of information must be covered, work backward to figure out the time sequence for teaching. Decide how long each practice should last and how many days a week to practice. In addition to fundamentals, rules, and defensive and offensive strategies, team plays, signs, and conditioning need to be scheduled.

Sample Checklist for Fundamentals

Baserunning
home to first
rounding bases
first to third
straight steals
double steals
squeeze home
hit and run
tagging on a fly ball
sliding
leadoffs
rundowns

Defense
pickoffs
rundowns
covering bases
backing up
cutoffs
infield depth
double plays
sacrifice situations
squeeze bunts
hit and run
steals
bunt situations
tagging runners
relays
first and third situations

Catcher
blocking dirt balls
throws to bases
blocking home
fielding throws
wild pitches and passed balls
foul pop flies
fielding bunts
dropped third strike
pickoffs and pitchouts
backing up first
basic stance
strategy
working with pitchers

Pitchers
delivery
covering home
fielding bunts and hits
pickoffs and pitchouts
target pitching
handling base runners
strategy

First Base
accepting throws
shifting
pop flies
fielding bunts and hits
double plays
cutoff position
dropped third strike
pickoffs

Second and Short
double plays
pickoffs
cutoffs and relays
covering second
fielding bunts and hits
drop steps
handling base runners
pop-ups
covering first

Third Base
fielding bunts and hits
pop-ups
handling base runners
pickoffs
drop steps
double plays
cutoffs
covering third

Outfield
do-or-die grounders
blocking grounders
drop step and arc
sun flies
communication
fence plays
diving catches
backing up
drifting
relays and cutoffs
crow hops
angle of pursuit

Offense
hitting drills
hitting off pitchers
strategy
bunting drills
bunting off pitchers
special plays

Conditioning
distance (foundation work)
sprints

Generally, in the first two weeks of a six-week practice period, individual skills should be emphasized. Team plays should be highlighted in the middle two weeks, and the final two weeks should be dominated by game situations and scrimmages but set your priorities according to the information at hand. Decide how much time is to be spent on offense, individual drills, team skills, and conditioning. Decide if chalk talks should take place in the classroom, on the field, or both.

No practice is set in concrete; problems may arise as the season progresses, and evaluations of players and the team's needs may change. However, never lose track of the time available in order to assure that priority information is always adequately covered. Some areas may have to be overlooked simply because time dictates such a decision. It is far better to have a team well schooled on a limited amount of information than superficially exposed to many areas.

The following examples describe three typical practice days from the first, third, and fifth weeks of practice.

Practice Day—First Week

2:30-2:50
Team stretch, run mile.

2:50-3:30
Drill series.

Infielders	**Pitchers**	**Outfielders**
overhand throw	overhand throw	overhand throw
quick throw (10)	snap throw (10)	crow hop
snap throw (10)	underhand toss	
underhand toss		
partner rundown	passed ball drill	hard grounders
shoulder toss	pop-ups	do-or-die grounders
drop steps	footwork to bases	point and throw
pickups	backup drill	
		easy flies
accepting throws	bunts	deep flies
grounders	grounders	

3:30-4:30
Offensive series
- Bunt progression drills
- Bunt off machine
- Agility drills
- Fence toss
- Batting-tee
- Jog and sprints.

3:30-4:05
Two starting pitchers workout
(10 minute warmup; 10 minute junk pitches; 10 minute target work).

3:50-4:30
Third pitcher works out
(same schedule).

4:30-5:00
Team defense
(rundowns).

5:00-
Conditioning
• four foul line runs (up and back equals one) at half speed
• ten sideline sprints at 3/4 speed
• six foul line runs; four at half speed, two at 3/4 speed.
Baserunning at full speed; five straight steals, five from first to third.

Practice Day—Third Week

2:30-3:00
Stretch, run mile, warm up arms.

3:00-3:30
Team works on rundown situations.
Two starting pitchers work out (drills, delivery work, targets).

3:30-4:30
Hitting off pitchers (two starters rotate every three outs; coach determines an out since a full team may not be on the field).
Players rotate from various stations in partners
• Fence
• Off machine
• Off pitchers
• Baserunning (five delays and five straight steals).
Coach hits flies/grounders between hits.

4:00-4:30
Third pitcher starts to work out.

4:30-5:00
Third pitcher throws to catcher.
Outfielders and extra players work on bunting.
Infielders work on bunt situations with base runners.

5:00-5:20
Conditioning series (same as before except distances are cut in half and speeds are increased).

1. **Individual skills should be emphasized.**

Practice Day—Fifth Week

2:30-3:00
Stretch, run mile, warm up arms.

3:00-3:30
Two starting pitchers warm up with catchers (typical series). Have team play a hitting game off machine (nine players set in each position; all extra players hit; catcher does not catch but handles plays at the plate; pitcher's position feeds the machine; hitters stay at bat as long as they hit safely; defense plays game situations with base runners; once a hitter makes an out she rotates into RF and everyone moves up one step; rotation is RF-CF-LF-3rd-SS-2nd-1st-P-C-hit). Can add competition for most hits, best defensive plays, etc.

3:30-4:30
Starting pitchers throw to hitters (pitchers rotate every three outs). Game situations; set defense; hitters run the bases; stop play as necessary to explain mistakes, etc.
Third pitcher warms up to throw for bunting on the sidelines.

4:30-5:00
First and third situations.

5:00-
Conditioning (three sets of circuits; first set as warmup, other sets at full speed).

The following chart depicts a sample six-week practice schedule. The same organizational principles apply, with the first two weeks covering individual drills, the second two weeks covering team plays, and the final two weeks covering game situations.

The sample is based on practice five days a week for approximately 2½ hours each day. It includes all the basic fundamentals, lectures on special areas (such as hitting, baserunning, bunting, strategy), conditioning, and sliding. A day off before the competition is scheduled to allow the players to be rested on the day of the game.

Practice During the Competitive Season

Practice during the competitive season is designed to sharpen skills. But remember, time off is important to keep players from getting bored with a routine. In a game, players should be mentally alert as well as physically prepared. Tough practices may be scheduled, but never just before a competition or just after a big road trip when the players are still recovering from traveling and playing.

In daily practices emphasize only those areas that seem most appropriate. For instance, if you are concentrating on offense,

The following code applies to the sample:

M: minutes	**IF**: infield	**LC**: lecture
DF: defense	**OF**: outfield	**EX**: exercises, stretching
LEC: lecture	**P**: pitcher	**ST**: situations
CON: conditioning	**GR**: grounders	**FL**: flies
WR: warm up arms	**DR**: drills	**BR**: baserunning
T: target work	**HT**: hitting	**BT**: bunting
THR: throwing	**STR**: strategy	**SIG**: signals

Sample Six Week Practice Schedule

	MONDAY	TUESDAY	WEDNESDAY	THURSDAY	FRIDAY
FIRST	20M—EX,CON 40M—THR series & DF 30M—HT LC 60M—HT series P—30M WR-T 20M—CON	20M—EX, CON 40M—THR & DF series 30M—BT LC 60M—BT, HT P —20M WR, 10M T 20M—CON	20M—EX, CON 40M—THR & DF 45M—IF HT OF DF P— 30M WR, T 20M—CON	20M—EX, CON 40M—THR & DF series 45M—OF HT IF DF P—30M WR, T 20M—CON	20M—EX, CON 40M—THR & DF series 30M—IF,OF DF P—WR, DR 60M—HT 20M—CON
SECOND	20M—EX,CON 30M—BR LC P—WR 45M—IF DF OF HT 45M—IF HT OF DF 15M—BR	20M—EX, CON 30M—DF ST P—WR, DR T 45M—OF DF IF HT 45M—OF HT IF DF 15M—BR	20M—EX, CON 30M—DF DR P—WR DR T 45M—OF DF IF HT 45M—OF DF IF HT 15M—BR	20M—EX, CON 30M—IF DF DR OF HT LC 30M—OF DF DR IF HT LC P—WR, DR T 30M—HT 15M—BR	20M—EX, CON 30M—DF DR P—WR, DR T 60M—HT, BR 15M—BR
THIRD	30M—EX, CON WR 30M—Rundown ST P—WR, T 60M—HT, GR & FL between 30M—BT ST 20M—CON	30M—EX,CON,WR 30M—1st & 3rd DF ST P—WR, T 30M—BT ST 60M—HT 20M—CON	30M—EX,CON,WR 30M—Relays, Cutoffs DF ST 30M—IF, OF FL & GR together P—WR, T 60M—HT 20M—CON	30M—EX,CON,WR 30M—pickoffs P—WR,T 30M—IF ST 60M—HT 20M—CON	30M—EX,CON,WR 30M—GR, FL P—WR,T 60M—HT 20M—CON 20M—Sliding
FOURTH	30M—EX,CON,WR 30M—DF review P—WR,T 60M—HT DF, ST 30M—IF & OF pop-ups 15M—CON	30M—EX,CON,WR 30M—DF review P—WR,T 60M—HT DF ST 30M—BT ST 15M—CON	30M—EX,CON,WR 30M—DF review P—WR,T 60M—HT DF ST 15M—CON 10M—Sliding	30M—EX,CON,WR 30M—DF review P—WR,T 60M—HT DF ST 20M—CON	30M—EX,CON,WR 30M—SIG & Rules 30M—GR, FL together 60M—HT 15M—CON
FIFTH	30M—EX,CON,WR 30M—HT game P—WR 60M—HT off P BR DR 30M—DF ST 15M—BR	30M—EX,CON,WR 30M—GR—FL P—WR 90M—game ST 15M—CON	30M—EX,CON,WR 30M—1st & 3rd ST P—WR 90M—game ST 15M—CON	30M—EX,CON,WR 30M—DF DR P—WR,T 90M—game ST 15M—CON	30M—EX,CON,WR 30M—GR, FL P—WR 60M—intra- squad game 10M—CON
SIXTH	30M—EX,CON,WR 30M—IF,OF DF together P—WR,T 30M—DF review 30M—HT game 10M—BR 10M—sliding	30M—EX,CON,WR 90M—pregame warmup intrasquad game with SIG 15M—CON	30M—EX,CON—WR 30M—DF LC review 60M—HT 15M—CON	30M—EX,CON,WR 30M—GR-FL SIG, review STR, rules 30M—IF, OF together 15M—CON	D A Y O F F

schedule hitting off pitchers, hitting off the machine, hitting drills for those players struggling at the plate, and some type of baserunning. Infielders and outfielders usually take 50 grounders or flies between offensive sessions.

During the week, mix up practices to cover throws to bases, relays, bunt situations, first and third situations, etc. If the players need to review fundamentals, take a day or part of a practice to run them through drills, but do so as an exception, not the rule.

Practice is not as structured during the competitive season because much depends on which weaknesses show up during a game, strategy changes that must be made, injuries, and the physical and mental state of the team. Have a general idea of which skills are to be covered at this time and then keep accurate notes on what is scheduled so that no area will be neglected. This is also an excellent time for players to suggest what they feel they need additional work on.

Coaches must depend on their own evaluation of the team's progress and what is learned from games to design the best practice for this time of year. The following is a sample practice day during the competitive season.

A Practice Day During the Competitive Season

2:30-3:00
Stretch, run mile, warm up arms.

3:00-4:00
Players rotate through offensive stations
- Off machine
- Off visiting pitcher
- Steals, first to second.

Coaches hit grounders and flies between hits.
Pitchers work 20 minutes on the sidelines (technique and targets).
Catchers then work on blocking dirt balls and throwdowns.

4:00-4:30
Review rundowns and first and third situations.

4:30-4:40
Ten minute run.

A Practice Schedule for Pitchers

The pitcher's schedule demands the most flexibility, because so much depends on the calibre of the pitcher, the condition she is in, and how much she has been throwing prior to the first day of practice. The progression is detailed later.

Pitchers should begin by working on delivery and timing, limiting their throwing to short (e.g. 20-minute) periods. By the second week, if their delivery is consistent, concentrate on building endurance and strength by throwing for longer periods and running. Then concentrate on target pitching, hitting the corners of the plate, working on various pitches, and pitching to batters. During the early phases the pitchers have more time to work on fielding drills, conditioning, and helping the catchers with their drills, which helps the catcher progress right along with the pitcher.

Pitchers gain endurance through conditioning and by developing consistency and accuracy, pitching with their entire body, not just their arm. Pitchers should throw for quality, not quantity. A concentrated workout of 20 minutes with specific objectives is much more productive than one hour of throwing batting practice. Pitchers should throw 20-minute sessions, building up to a maximum of three 20-minute sessions (pitchers throw between three and five pitches a minute, so one session equals about 60 pitches). There should always be a purpose to practice, and supervision is very important. A session may cover delivery, a type of pitch, a location, a corners game, etc.

Don't overuse pitchers against hitters in a practice situation, but when pitchers do throw, they should pitch competitively. Pitchers never throw for a hitter's benefit. They should be instructed to work for the groundout, the pop-up, the strikeout, and to always hit the corners. The catcher or one of the coaches should call balls and strikes.

How quickly a pitcher moves through the progression varies. The lower-skilled pitcher will have to spend more time working on her delivery. The highly skilled pitcher will quickly advance to target work and will be throwing against hitters in a short time. A pitcher who can't hit her targets has no business throwing to hitters or working on junk pitches. As is true for other players, during the competitive season the pitchers only throw enough to keep sharp. Also continue conditioning and defensive skill work. Bring in local pitchers (men or women) to help out at practice.

The following example is a typical pitcher's progression for someone who has not been throwing in the off-season. Increase the time for those who come into spring practice ready to throw.

	M	T	W	TH	F
1st week	20	20	20	20	20
2nd week	10-10	10-10	10-10	20-10	20-10
3rd week	20-10	20-10	20-10	20-10	20-10
4th week	20-20	20-20-20	20-20	20-20-20	20-20
5th week	20-20-20	20-20	20-20-20	20-20	20-20-20
6th week	20-20-20	20-20-20	20-20	20	day off

Sample Pitcher's Progression Chart
(minutes per day)

During the fifth and sixth weeks, combine the practice times for the two starting pitchers. Have them both throw for a 60-minute session, alternating against hitters after every three outs. This simulation of a game situation is very beneficial.

A typical daily practice for pitchers is detailed below, showing changes through the progression. The usual 15 minutes of stretching exercises precede each workout.

Sample Daily Progressions

PHASE 1
Ten minutes—run
Ten minutes—overhand throw
Five minutes—additional arm stretches
Twenty minutes—work on delivery
Five minutes—break
Fifteen minutes—helping catcher (blocking, pop-ups)
Fifteen minutes—defense (bunts, pop-ups, pickoffs)
Ten minutes—run
Join team in hitting

PHASE 2
One — mile run
Ten minutes—overhand warmup and drills
Ten minutes—work on delivery
Five minutes—break
Twenty minutes—target work
Ten minutes—grounders
One — mile run
Join team in hitting

PHASE 3
One — mile run
Ten minutes—overhand throw and drills
Sixty minutes—pitch to hitters (alternating with second pitcher)
Ten minutes—hitting
One — mile run

Sample Week During Competition

Monday—off
Tuesday—20 minutes on delivery
Wednesday—20-20 to hitters
Thursday—20 minutes on any problem areas
Friday—off
Saturday—game

Pitcher: Game Preparation

Pitchers should establish a pattern of procedures before each game. Just as in practice, they should stretch and run to warm up. If the pitcher also hits, she should take batting practice early.

The pitcher's actual warmup should be timed to finish just before the game begins. She should take approximately seven minutes to warm up overhand, 10 minutes of work on delivery and various pitches, and 10 minutes on target work (strikes, waste pitches, pitchouts). The pitcher and catcher should be isolated from the rest of the team and certainly from the crowd to assure the maximum amount of mental concentration. Both the catcher and the coach help prepare the pitcher, mentally and physically, for a game.

In high school situations, often there is little time for a warmup. Players might be released from school 30 minutes before game time, and when fields are located off campus it is very difficult to schedule a proper warmup before game time. For that reason, young pitchers should spend a lot of time perfecting their delivery. For the average pitcher, developing a consistent delivery is the first and most important step. The inability to pitch strikes (on the corners) is the biggest downfall of the average pitcher. Take it one step at a time—delivery and natural speed, targets, and then a variety of pitches.

2. Players should stretch and run to warm up.

Stretching & Conditioning

Every team needs a consistent and thorough exercise program. One of the best is a static exercise program developed by Robert A. Anderson. (His book *Stretching* can be ordered through Stretching, Inc., P.O. Box 767, Palmer Lake, CO, 80133.) The program is aimed at relaxing the muscles, making them limber and less prone to injury. All the exercises are based on stretching various muscles and holding positions from 20 seconds to one minute until the muscles stop resisting and start slowly relaxing and stretching fully. Each position is held still because bouncing or jerking only adds to the muscles' tension. Anderson developed a program for baseball that can be adopted easily for softball.

Well-conditioned athletes perform better for longer periods of time. Consequently, every training program should include distance work, as a foundation for overall conditioning, and sprints, which is what most softball movements are. If in doubt, ask a track specialist to recommend a good program. The following provides a variety of methods that can be used to condition softball players. (Players should understand that the mile run is not a race, but an individual warmup. Each athlete should run at her own pace and keep track of her times, improving each week.)

Distance Work

- Run a mile.
- Run for a set amount of time.
- Run from one foul line to the other, across the widest part of the field (vary speeds).
- Jog in a line for a set distance or period of time. On signal, the last person in line sprints to the front.

Sprint Work

- Sixty-foot sprints (along the sidelines).
- Circuits (vary speeds).
- Jog and sprint (jog 60 feet, then sprint 60 feet; three sets of five, up and back equals one).
- Steals (to any base).
- Leadoffs.
- Chase game. Start with a player at each base and one at the midpoint between each base. On signal everyone starts running the bases, trying to catch the player ahead.
- Get-back drill. (Everyone starts at first base. One coach is at first and another is at third. One player acts as a base runner at first. She takes her leadoff and is told by the coach to get back to the base because of a pickoff attempt. Then, as if the imagined throw goes into the outfield, she is told to race to second, where the third base coach tells her to continue to third. Just as she rounds second, the coach changes her mind and tells her to return to second. On a second imagined overthrow she is told that now she can come to third. The same process is carried through until she reaches home. The next runner starts as the runner ahead of her heads for third base. This teaches the runners to run at full speed.
- Doubles. Set half the team at home plate and half at second. Those in line wait behind the bag and out of the way. The runner at home starts the drill by running a double. After she crosses second, one of the runners at second takes off, running a double to home. Run for either a set time or specific number of sets.
- Bunt and run, third to home. Half the runners are at first and half are at third. The runners at first execute a bunt and run, running at full speed from first to third. Runners at third practice leadoffs and then sprint home at full speed, acting as they would on a hit. Base on time or set of sprints.
- Partner sprint race. Everyone has a partner. Set a distance, such as 60 feet. The players race to a spot and then return, at which time their partners take off. Continue for a number of sets.
- Agility drills (check with other coaches for suggestions).

3. Most softball movements are sprints.

Conditioning Within Practice

Outfield

- Foul line flies. Players all start in left field on the foul line. A coach hits a fly ball to left field that the player catches and throws to third. The player then runs to center field, where a second fly is hit. The throw goes to second. The player continues to right field, where the final fly ball is hit. The throw is made to first or second. The player moves to the right field foul line and the next player starts out in left field.
- Outfield suicide. Three players are positioned in the outfield. Two or three infielders are used to cover bases. All other players are at home to hit off the machine, which is set on the pitching rubber. Every ball hit is the outfielders' responsibility. Infielders only cover bases or handle relays. Hitters run the bases as usual, but no steals. Add a catcher for throws to home.
- Pass drill. Use a softball or football. The players line up on a foul line and are set in groups of three or four. The first group jogs to the coach, hands her the ball, then sprints toward the other foul line, looking for the ball. The coach throws the ball to one of them. After crossing the foul line the group turns around and repeats the process on the way back. If a football is used, add defensive players so that when players go out for a pass there is both a receiver and defensive player. It is good competition and players forget about the hard work.

Infield

- Ten in a row. Each infielder is hit 10 balls, one almost immediately after the other. Hit a variety of balls and give the fielder just enough time to return to her original position. All throws are to home plate.
- Pickup circuit. Starting at home plate, partners face each other across the baseline and toss grounders back and forth as they move from home to first. Players can run a home run or an actual circuit.
- Rundowns.
- First and third situations.
- Pop-ups and foul balls. Set all the infielders in their positions, including a pitcher and catcher. Hit pop flies in random order, allowing the fielders just enough time to return to their original positions. Except for the pitcher and catcher all other players should be either attempting to catch the ball or covering a base on every hit.

3

Hitting
Fundamentals

This section deals with the specific fundamentals of hitting and offers selected drills and games to develop the skills. In fastpitch softball, it is very important to develop a quick, compact swing. The principles of top-hand hitting, the finger grip, and bat acceleration are the foundations for this hitting system.

Stance
The stance should be comfortable, with personal preference playing a major role. The feet are at least shoulder-width apart. The stride should be 6 to 12 inches with the left toe slightly turned out (open).

Bat Position
Hold bat behind the right ear and off the back shoulder. Bat position can vary in the initial stance, but the bat should be held in front of the body, not laid back across the shoulder or wrapped around the head.

4. Normal batting stance.

Grip

Use a finger grip (like a golf grip) in which the bat is held in the fingers, not in the hand. This grip covers more of the bat handle, which increases bat control and facilitates top-hand hitting. Lay the bat across the fingers of the left hand, angling the handle from the base of the little finger to the tip of the first finger. Then wrap the left hand around the handle, maintaining the angle and creating a "V" by pointing the thumb and first finger toward the right shoulder. Maintaining these same angles, wrap the fingers of the right hand around the bat handle, but do not interlock the little fingers. Keep a light grip. The left hand simply holds the bat. The right hand initiates and directs the bat power.

5-8. Gripping the bat.

5. Lay bat handle across left hand.

6. Grip of left hand.

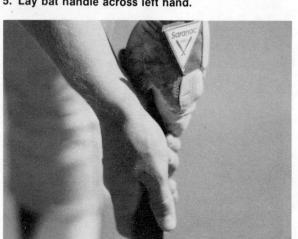

7. Grip of right hand.

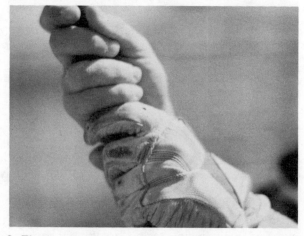

8. The finger grip.

Inward Rotation

Inward rotation refers to the cocking action of the arms and hands made just as the stride is taken. Just before the swing, the left hand pushes the bat directly back, straightening out the left arm. If no stride is taken, inward rotation should be initiated at some point before the pitch is released.

Back Elbow

Too much emphasis has been placed on the position of the back elbow. It should be held in a comfortable position, but not tucked to the body.

9-10. Inward rotation.

9. Begin inward rotation.   **10. Straighten out the left arm.**

Top Hand

The top hand is the power hand, the dominant hand in the swing. Hitters should be told to throw the right hand (top hand) at the ball.

Arm Extension

The arms should be fully extended on contact. Do not start the swing by extending the arms and then sweeping across the plate; instead, throw the hands out at the ball.

11. Throw the top hand at the ball.

Left Shoulder

The left shoulder should be pointed at the ball until the hands explode out to make contact and should open up on the follow-through, not initiate the swing. Hitters often open their left shoulder as they rotate their upper body to start the swing, pulling their hands through the plate instead of leading with their hands and the head of the bat. This mistake most often occurs on an inside pitch, where the batter pulls her body away from the ball instead of hitting the pitch 2½-3 feet in front of the plate. When the left shoulder is pulled out, the head follows.

Head

The head should be kept virtually still throughout the swing. As the hands accelerate to the ball, the head flexes forward to maintain eye contact during the swing.

Swing

Since line drives and ground balls are the highest percentage hits, batters should chop down on the ball, rather than take a level or uppercut swing. Even on a high strike a hitter can come down on top of the ball.

12. **Chop down on a low pitch.**

13. **Chop a high pitch.**

Bat Acceleration

Bat acceleration is vital in hitting. Hitters should never time the ball or guide their bat. The batter should wait until the last possible second, then explode on the ball, throwing her top hand at the pitch. This technique allows the hitter to wait until the pitch is near the plate to determine if it is a ball or strike. It also helps against a pitcher with an odd motion or good change-up and stops the hitter from slowing her swing against average and slow pitchers.

The Hitting Diagonal

Never hit the ball on top of the plate. Hit the inside pitch three feet in front of the plate. Hit the pitch coming across the middle of the plate 1-1½ feet in front of the plate, and hit the outside pitch just over the outside corner of the plate.

Hitting the Ball Where It Is Pitched

A hitter should always be aggressive, but she should not try to pull every pitch. Using the principles of the hitting diagonal, the hitter should drive the outside pitch to the opposite field with maximum bat speed and arm extension. Balls pitched down the middle of the plate should be hit right back up the middle. The hitter must recognize the inside pitch early, in order to hit it way out in front of the plate and pull it.

14. Hit a low inside pitch three feet in front of the plate.

15. Chop a high, inside pitch.

Hitting Drills

Fence Drill

A tosser stands to the side and in front of a hitter (at a 45-degree angle) and tosses balls, varying the spot at which the ball is thrown. The batter reacts to each toss, hitting the ball into a reinforced fence. (If a fence is not available, the same drill can be set up in the outfield, but it demands more space and time.) The tosser should give the hitter plenty of time between pitches so that the batter can aggressively attack each pitch with the maximum amount of concentration on fundamentals. To prevent the batter from timing the toss, the tosser should occasionally fake a toss to see if the hitter moves her hands forward, hitches, or shifts her weight prematurely.

Tire Drill

Hang a tire or attach it firmly to a post and cut a horizontal slice through it. The hitter must swing her bat through the cut portion of the tire. Move the hitter (or tire) around to simulate inside and outside pitches. This drill helps teach hitters bat extension and optimal velocity.

16. Hit a low, outside pitch over the corner of the plate. **17.** Chop a high, outside pitch.

Batting Tee

The batting tee is an excellent tool for teaching hitting fundamentals. In a controlled situation it helps the hitter learn to keep her head still, to hit various pitches, and to accelerate the bat while maintaining control of her body. Each swing is at full speed.

Shadow Drill

This drill will detect lunging in a hitter. Have a hitter stand with the sun to her back so that the shadow of her head and body is projected on the ground directly in front of her. Have the hitter take her normal stance. Mark where the shadow of her head hits the ground. After the hitter takes her normal swing, mark where the shadow of her head ends up. Hitters who lunge at the ball will move their head forward as much as 2 feet. Even after a hard cut, the shadow of the head should move only a little, because the head remains still throughout the swing. The hitter has to learn to rotate over her hips instead of lunging forward.

Line Drives

Hitters toss balls to themselves and try to hit line drives and grounders across the outfield to their partners. Emphasize tossing the ball out in front of the plate and arm extension.

Hip Turns

Have the hitters place a bat across their lower back or hip and hold it there by placing the inside of their wrists against the bat at either end (may use wrists or hands). Tell the hitters to "hit the ball with their hips," turning the bat and hip as they swing. It should be a quick motion. This will help teach hip rotation and pivoting on the toes.

Fist Punch

The hitter takes a normal stance without a bat and makes a fist with her right hand in the approximate area that she would hold a bat (off the right shoulder). Her left arm is by her side. Visualizing an inside pitch, the hitter throws her fist directly across her body as if she were throwing a punch at someone. This should be a quick, aggressive movement. Keep the left shoulder still at first, then open it on the follow-through. This drill helps hitters who tend to straighten their arms too soon and sweep swing across the plate instead of throwing their hands (and bat head) out at the ball.

Repetitions

The hitter takes a normal stance with her bat. She takes as many swings (always using good form) as she can in a 10-second period. The hitter can also do a predetermined number (five) in so many sets (three) to accomplish the same results.

Throwing the Bat

Saw off the knob of a wooden bat and set the hitter in the outfield, far away from everyone. Tell the hitter to take a normal cut and release the bat at the point of imagined contact with the ball. If the hitter uses her top hand and proper extension, the bat will fly straight out from the hitter, like a ball hit down the middle. If the hitter is dragging the bat with her bottom hand, the bat will fly to the left.

Swinging the Bat

A hitter with a bat imagines different pitches thrown to her and swings her bat accordingly. This can also be done in slow motion to emphasize feeling the proper swing, but the hitter should always end this drill with good, hard cuts. Emphasize proper form at all times.

Isometrics

The hitter lays the head of the bat against a pole or similar solid object and applies pressure. In one series, have the hitter stand near and just in front of the pole, placing the head of the bat against the pole, with her arms bent in a flexed position. In another series, have the hitter stand farther away from the pole, extend her arms fully, and apply pressure to the head of the bat. This drill will help develop wrist, forearm, and biceps strength.

Machines

Machines are a great tool if used properly, but hitters should never time a machine. Vary the time used to feed each pitch so that the hitters will have to react to the ball. Don't set the machine to throw balls over the center of the plate (unless the hitter is still working on basic fundamentals), but move the location to work on various pitches. Try hitting baseballs early in the season to force the hitters to concentrate even more on the smaller ball.

Hitting Games

- During practice keep track of all solid hits and post the information to help create team competition.
- Play a mini-game off a pitching machine. The hitter stays at bat as long as she hits safely. When she makes an out, she rotates into a defensive position (RF-CF-LF-3rd-SS-2nd-1st-P-hit). The coach may also take over the pitching position.
- In another mini-game, make up teams (infield vs. outfield) and set up a point system. Record one point for hard hits, two points for safe hits, three points for extra-base hits, etc. The team with the most points recorded is rewarded in some way.
- Instead of rotating based on the number of swings, have each batter take a set number of times at the plate (at bats). Keep track

of the hits. It should be a game situation with a complete defense and several hitters so that there is time between at bats. Post the results. Anyone who fails to make good contact or get a hit must run extra laps.

- Assign two teams. Instead of rotating each inning after every three outs, rotate after every player on a team gets one time at bat. Count the hits and runs scored. The game can be played for a specific amount of time or innings.

18. **Drive a high, outside pitch to the opposite field.**

4

Hitting with the Mind

When it comes to developing a skill, such as hitting, the focus is usually on fundamentals. The responsibility for success is placed entirely on technique without considering such other factors as picking the right pitch to hit, playing the count, and knowing the pitcher. Hours of practice are devoted to proper fundamentals, and so it should be, but the other factor that plays a vital role—the mental side of hitting—must be studied just as intently.

Rod Carew is a professional baseball player who has developed his own science of hitting. Carew studies each pitcher and changes his stance and bat to fit the pitcher's style. Most hitters, however, keep a favorite bat and spend a lifetime finding a comfortable stance. Still, there are very few Mickey Mantles, Ted Williams, Pete Roses, or George Bretts.

To be the best hitter possible, an athlete must invest as much time on the mental aspects as on the physical fundamentals. Very few athletes reach their potential on physical ability alone. The intelligent player knows her own strengths and weaknesses and beats opponents with her mind as well as her natural ability.

The Right Pitch

Hitters should know themselves and study their opponent, the pitcher. Speaking in terms of the fastball, every player should know which pitch she hits best and which pitch gives her the most problem. Hitters should know if they are good high-ball hitters or low-ball hitters, and if they do best on the inside or outside pitches. When a player knows which pitches she hits best, she can look for those pitches and lay off the pitches she has problems with.

Ted Williams made a chart of all the pitches that could come over the strike zone. He calculated what his batting average would be for each of these locations. For instance, if all he could hit were low and away pitches he would bat only .230, but if he could hit all inside belt-high strikes he would hit .360. Correctly deciding which pitch to hit is where the intelligent hitter beats the reaction hitter. The question is not just whether a pitch is a ball or a strike, but whether it is the right pitch for the hitter to hit. It is important that every hitter know her best pitch and look for it. If the pitcher makes a mistake, the hitter must be ready to take advantage of it.

Of course, if a hitter has two strikes against her, she should be concerned with any pitch that is around the strike zone—her options are too limited to wait for just the right pitch.

Picking the right pitch applies to junk pitches as well as the fastball. Very few pitchers today rely strictly on a fastball. Most have at least one or two other strong pitches, such as a change-up, rise, drop, curve, or some combination thereof.

The smart batter anticipates a certain pitch and decides well in advance how to handle that pitch. For instance, if a pitcher has a reputation as a rise-ball pitcher, which in 90 percent of the cases means she's depending on a pitch that is not thrown for a strike, a hitter can decide to lay off the high pitch and force that pitcher to bring the pitch down in the strike zone. If the pitcher is unable to make an adjustment, she may find herself behind in the count with the advantage going to the hitter.

Knowing the Pitcher

Sometimes a coach is able to develop a scouting report on a pitcher, but each athlete should make it her responsibility to study the pitcher. Ideally, a hitter should watch a pitcher against another team, but usually a hitter gets only "on the job" training. This is why a hitter should study the game while on the bench. Further, players should exchange information on the speed of the pitcher and the location or type of pitches being thrown. After the first couple of innings, it's important to meet as a team to discuss the pitcher and define a team strategy.

The hitter should know which pitch the pitcher throws most often, which is her best pitch, what she throws on the first pitch, what her strikeout pitch is, and if she has any pattern for the location or type of pitch she throws. The more the hitter knows about the pitcher and which pitch to look for in a given situation, the better her chances are at the plate. Play the percentages.

A good example is a pitcher who relies strictly on a rise-drop combination. The rise is thrown for a ball, whereas the drop is a strike about half the time. In this case, the hitter would stay off the high pitch and be selective on the drop. If the strategy works, the pitcher is forced to stay with one pitch or get behind in the count, and the hitter can concentrate on low strikes. A quality pitcher will adjust, probably by starting to throw high fastball strikes, but there are many successful pitchers who have a difficult time changing what has been effective for them.

A hitter should also determine whether a pitcher likes to get ahead in the count right away or likes to play around with the hitters, trying to make them go for a bad pitch. Some pitchers throw their first pitch virtually down the middle of the plate, relying on a hitter's failure to swing at early pitches. When a quality pitcher faces a strong hitter she will try to get ahead in the count, at which point she will stay away from strikes and tease the hitter with borderline pitches that the batter can't afford to let go by. With either pitcher, the hitter must be aggressive and get on the offense early to try to dictate the pattern.

On the other hand, if the pitcher uses more junk pitches and tries to tease the hitter early by staying around the corners, the hitter must be more cautious. The hitter must let the pitcher know she is in control and will only go for strikes. Once a pitcher finds a hitter who has no bat discipline, she will never throw a strike.

Playing the Count

The count plays a very important role in the hitting game. The first pitch starts off the game and can be very crucial. Coaches hate to see hitters get behind in the count by taking the first strike (with the possible exception of the first time a hitter faces the pitcher or if the pitcher is having control problems). A hitter should always be ready the minute she steps into the batter's box, and if the first pitch is the right pitch, it should never go by untouched.

19. A hitter should always be alert.

As long as the hitter is ahead of the count (2-0, 2-1, 3-0, 3-1) she can afford to be choosy. When holding the upper hand, the hitter should be twice as alert for her pitch and never consider a walk. Make the pitcher come to the hitter with "her pitch." The batter will take a walk if it is given, but she should never lose her concentration by relaxing too much and expecting a walk.

It's common practice on a 3-0 count for the hitter to be looking all the way. Some pitchers even rely on that tradition to throw a sure strike, which is a great pitch to hit. If a hitter displays poor bat discipline, it's good strategy to make the pitcher come to the plate, but if an excellent hitter is at the plate, it is a good opportunity to hit away if it's "the right pitch."

Presence and Attitude

Influence or strategy manuevers between the hitter and pitcher are present in every game. Hitters try to convince pitchers that the pressure is on them to throw strikes and pitchers try to convince hitters that they are in charge because only they know which pitch is coming. Some hitters will try to influence the pitcher to throw particular pitches.

One reason black-and-white rules about how to pitch certain hitters (based primarily on their stance) don't hold true is because they fail to take into account individual hitter's traits. For instance, when a hitter crowds the plate the traditional strategy is to jam the hitter with an inside fastball, but some hitters crowd the plate looking for that pitch and have the quick hands and physical ability to hit that pitch well. Similarly, if a hitter hits outside pitches well, she can try backing off the plate to see if the catcher will call for an outside target. If a pitcher has a change-up and the hitter hits those well, but has trouble handling the fastball, she can act anxious at the plate or overswing at the first pitch. Of course, the more a team has been scouted, the less these tricks will be effective.

Umpires

Every hitter would like to go to the plate confident that balls and strikes will be called correctly, but often the most that can be hoped for is consistent tendencies. Even if the hitter disagrees with the umpire's strike zone, the zone can be tolerated if it is consistent. The trouble comes when the umpire has not made up her mind on balls and strikes. Nothing frustrates a hitter more than an umpire that changes the strike zone each inning, gets tired late in the game, or gets strike happy. In these cases the only thing that will help the hitter is a good attitude. When faced with an inconsistent umpire, the hitter can't afford to play too many tricks or be choosy about balls and strikes, and above all she must stay aggressive.

A good hitter never lets an umpire take the bat out of her hand. The batter must learn to channel her frustrations into improving her concentration to hit the ball. Losing control will only make matters worse. Hitters can never let the umpire—or worse yet, the pitcher—know she is upset.

General Comments

Every hitter needs to work hard in practice to develop the best possible fundamentals, which are the foundation of hitting. Batters must develop a correct, consistent swing that gives them confidence. From there the burden of success rests inside the athlete.

Every hitter should know her own strengths and weaknesses and study the mental aspects of hitting. Pitch selection—knowing the right pitch to hit—is a vital concept. If a coach has a choice between a hitter with great ability who depends on reaction alone and a hitter with strong fundamentals who is intelligent, most will select the smart player. Further, the more a coach trusts a hitter's judgment, the more freedom she will give that athlete.

If technique were all that mattered, there would be many highly successful textbook coaches and athletes. However, the attitude of each athlete and her ability to learn about herself and play an intelligent game makes a significant impact on her success.

20. Know the right pitch to hit.

Angle Bunting off the Pivot

The traditional view of bunting shows the bunter squared around, with her body completely facing the pitcher and the bat held parallel to the ground. Angle bunting refers to the 45-degree angle at which the bat is to be held. The purpose is simply to eliminate pop-ups. Pivot bunting allows a smooth and quick transition from the hitting position to the bunting position to prepare for a fast start out of the box after the bunt.

    The following explanation is based on the sacrifice bunt. The same rules apply on a drag bunt, except that the bunter waits longer before initiating any movement and must make the proper adjustments to get a quick jump out of the box on contact with the ball.

21. **Body position in front of the box.**

Body Position
- Stand in front of the box.
- Pivot on the balls of the feet, shifting 75 percent of the weight to the front foot.
- Drop the bat to a 45-degree angle.
- Bring the head of the bat forward just in front of the face.
- Bend and relax the knees.
- Position the left foot very close to the plate.

Bat Position

- Hold the bat at a 45-degree angle at all times.
- The bat should be in front of the plate.
- The bat should cover the entire plate.

Hand Position

- Hold the top hand a little more than halfway up the bat.
- Both hands can be moved up the bat or can be split.
- Hold the hands away from the body.
- Bend the elbows, with the bat approximately one-half arm length away from the body.
- Hold the bat loosely with the top hand so as not to give too much resistance when the ball hits the bat.

Head Position

- Hold the head almost directly behind the bat.
- Watch the ball hit the bat.

Comments: The bunter should be in the front part of the batter's box to give her the maximal amount of fair territory. The bunter should stand close to the plate (left foot forward for a right-handed hitter) so that she can cover the entire plate with her bat from a relaxed position. This minimizes bat movement, gives the bunter a clear perspective of the strike zone, and allows her to see the ball clearly as it comes to the plate. Traditionally, the head was above the bat, but in angle bunting the head is almost directly behind the bat, providing the best possible view of the ball in relation to the bat.

22-23. Angle bunt position.

22. Front view shows hand, bat and head position.

23. Side view shows elbows bent and bat held away from body.

Direction of the Bunt

- Direct the bunt with the bottom hand. Many bunters direct the ball with the top hand, but the resistance that exists with a tight right (top)-hand grip causes the ball to jump off the bat since the bunter is actually punching the ball, not bunting it.
- To place the ball down the first base line, push the bottom hand out and away from the body, always maintaining the bat angle.
- To place the ball down third, pull the bottom half of the bat toward the body, keeping the proper angle.

Comments: A bunter must have soft hands. A typical bunting error is to grip the bat too tightly and attack the ball, rather than maintaining the proper angle and letting the ball simply drop off the bat. Using the bottom hand to direct the bat will help the bunter relax the top hand.

Bat Movement

- Keep the bat at a 45-degree angle at all times.
- On the low strike, bend the knees and bring the body to the proper level, keeping the bat angle the same.
- On the high strike, raise the body and keep the proper angle.
- For an inside strike, move the hands to the inside corner of the plate and make sure the hands are in front of the body and plate.
- For an outside pitch, move the hands over the outside corner of the plate and bunt the ball just in front of the plate.

Comments: One of the most neglected fundamentals of bunting is proper use of the body. The hands should move only slightly around

24. Bunt down third base line.

25. Bunt down first base line.

the plate, while the body must adjust to the pitch. Further, if a hitter has a normal stance, with her feet close together, she will have to widen that stance and place her back foot slightly behind her front foot when she bunts to allow for proper body positioning.

General Rules of Bunting

- When sacrificing, square around early enough to be in the bunting position just as the ball is released by the pitcher. The faster the pitcher, the sooner the bunter must start her motion. Never wait so long that the bunt is rushed. In a sacrifice bunt the body should be still upon contact with the ball. Don't be moving from the hitting position as contact is made with the ball.
- Based on how the defense is aligned, decide before bunting where the best location for the bunt is and adjust to that angle. Generally speaking, inside strikes are easier to bunt down third whereas outside strikes lend themselves to bunts down first.
- The 45-degree angle eliminates pop-ups since the ball comes off the top portion of the bat and will take off directly behind the hitter, toward the backstop.
- The hands should be away and in front of the body, but the arms should not be fully extended. With the elbows bent, the bat should be held about one-half arm's length away from the body.
- The proper bunting position should give the bunter a clear picture of balls and strikes. Be selective.

Comments: Bunting is one of the easiest skills in softball when the proper fundamentals are practiced. The bat is simply an extension of the arm. Bunting is like catching the ball with the right hand (for the right-handed batter).

26. Drag bunt down first base line.

A Progression for Teaching Angle Bunting

- Lecture on proper fundamentals and philosophy behind the style.
- Demonstrate the proper techniques.
- Give each team member a bat and cover the following.
  1. Angle and grip.
  2. Position of hands to the body.
  3. Position of head to the bat.
  4. Body positioning with the pivot.
  5. Relation of the body to the plate (draw or use a home plate).
- Drill the team on converting from the batting to the bunting stance.
  1. Have each player assume a batting stance. On signal everyone drops to the proper bunting position as quickly as possible. Repeat 30 times, correcting mistakes as they are made.
  2. Using the same drill, call out where the pitch is located (inside, low, outside, high) and watch the hand position and body movement. Pay special attention to low pitches because bunters tend to drop the head of the bat, losing the desired angle.
- Break the team into partners with no bats.
  1. One partner tosses the ball to another, who acts as the bunter. For the first 25 bunts have the bunter already squared around so that all she has to do is concentrate on catching the ball. On low pitches watch to see if the ball is caught with the palm down. If the bunter rotates her hand (palm up, fingers down) for the low pitch, that will translate into dropping the head of the bat.
  2. In the next set have the bunter start in a batting stance, then drop into the bunting stance and again catch the ball.
- Make up several groups of five for actual bunting practice. Have one player toss the ball to a bunter, who uses a bat. Extra people field the ball. In the first session, the bunter squares around immediately; later she starts in the batting position.
- The team is now ready for game situations. After the players consistently display the proper fundamentals in drills, have them progress to bunting off machines and pitchers. Drill heavily to ensure that the players develop good habits and can assume the proper positioning by just reacting.

6

Baserunning

Good baserunning techniques are vital to a successful offense. Base runners must be aggressive, should always run at full speed, must think a base ahead, and should be aware of where the ball is at all times. Baserunners should use their own judgment when running the bases, and depend upon the coaches' directions when unsure or when the ball cannot be easily located while running.

Generally speaking, the third base coach is responsible for giving signals. The hitter/baserunner should immediately look to third base after she reaches first base and should check back after each pitch or play. The third base coach will help, through arm signals and voice commands, as the runner tries to advance from first to third, second to third, second to home, and third to home. The first base coach will help the runner going from home to first or second and from first to second. The first base coach is also responsible for watching for pickoffs, making sure the base runner at first is fully aware of the situation, and repeating signals from the third base coach if there is any confusion.

27. Run at full speed.

Baserunners Should Know:
* Number of outs.
* Inning.
* Score.
* Defensive alignment.
* Strength of the outfielder's arm.
* Strength of the catcher's arm.
* If the team has a pickoff play.
* What kind of jump to get.
* Signals.
* Where the ball is at all times.
* Speed of the baserunner ahead of her.

General Rules
* Locate the ball whenever possible.
* When a sudden stop is needed, always slide.
* When in doubt, always slide.
* Always look a base ahead to see if anyone is covering, especially on a bunt or fake bunt.
* Never hesitate, always run hard.
* When rounding bases, run in a flat arc and hit the base with the left foot (on the inside of the base), but don't break stride to accomplish this.
* When attempting to beat out an infield hit, don't lunge or jump to reach first base. Instead, lean into the bag like a track runner hitting the finish line.
* When there are two runners on base and the second (or trailing) runner gets caught between bases, the second runner should get into a rundown.
* Always take a lead directly in the baseline. The shortest distance between two points is a straight line.
* Notice where the fielders are playing and where the throw will be coming from so that the slide will be to the opposite side.
* When a play is being made on another baserunner, as in a throw to home from the outfield, advance another base if possible.
* When running to a base, for example from second to third, don't slow down before getting to the base. Instead, continue to run hard until instructed by the coach to stop, then quickly apply the brakes. Baserunners who automatically slow down as they approach a base often lose the opportunity to advance another base.
* With two outs and a full count on the batter, the runner takes off with the pitch.

Specific Rules
* When a first baseman retreats up the line toward first as if to make a pickoff play, the baserunner should shorten her lead and then dive and slide back to the bag if the pickoff is on. The exception is if the runner wants to steal second on the attempt.

- When on second with no outs, the baserunner should always tag on a fly ball.
- When on second with one out, the baserunner should always go halfway.
- When on third with no outs, the baserunner should always make sure the ball goes through the infield before she leaves her bag, and she should tag on all fly balls. The exception is the high chopper, when the runner should automatically run for home.
- When there are runners on second and third, the runner at third should always try to score on a ground ball.
- When a ball is hit, make sure it is a grounder or is hit through the infield before taking off. This hesitation will help avoid double plays caused when a baserunner takes off too soon and a line drive is hit right at an infielder.

The Leadoff

The most common leadoff technique is a running or one-way lead, but the most efficient method is the controlled lead. The controlled lead allows the runner to get the maximal distance with her lead while maintaining continuous body control. Upon concluding the leadoff, the runner will be in a position to move in either direction at a moment's notice, depending upon whether the ball is hit or a pickoff attempt is made. The following is a step-by-step explanation of the control lead.

28-33. The controlled lead.

28. Step with the right foot.

29. Crossover.

The runner assumes a relaxed stance by the bag, with her feet no more than shoulder-width apart. Instead of placing her foot on top of the base, she places the side of her left foot against the side of the bag. Keeping both feet at the same level increases stability and makes it easier for the runner to push off the dirt and bag.

To initiate movement, the runner starts with a short step with her right foot approximately 1½ feet in a direct line toward the next base. Keeping her shoulders square to the infield, she uses a crossover step with her left leg and a hard swinging action of her arms to propel her body the maximal distance. At the conclusion of the leadoff the runner comes down with her feet farther than shoulder-width apart, her knees slightly bent, and in a stable position. The following are general rules concerning leadoffs.

- Always get the biggest lead possible.
- Unless otherwise instructed the lead should be made so the baserunner is always thinking about getting back to the bag on a pickoff or line drive.
- If the first baseman plays close to first, the runner there must shorten her lead.
- A shorter lead at first is also required when a left-handed pull hitter is at bat, in order to avoid the double play on a sharply hit line drive to the first or second baseman.
- Baserunners should keep their eyes on the ball as much as possible. The runner should never turn her back on anyone holding the ball, especially the pitcher or catcher.

30. Crossover.

31. Land.

- When a fly ball is hit, the baserunner should immediately retreat to her bag, but keep watching the ball in case it is misplayed or an errant throw that allows her to advance a base is made. The exception is when there are two outs, in which case the runner takes off with the hit.
- Leadoffs should be taken in foul territory when taken at third base.

Teaching baserunning involves lecturing on proper techniques, philosophy, and practice. However, there is no substitute for running the bases, either in drills listed in the conditioning chapter or in game situations. The most effective drill for teaching baserunning is a simulated game situation that has a coach on the pitching rubber (throwing strikes over the plate), a hitter at the plate, and a couple of base runners at first base, with a coach who watches their fundamentals.

The coach acting as the pitcher tells a situation to the batter (sacrifice, hit and run, bunt and run, etc.), and the batter must execute the proper offensive skills. The runner must then execute the play and react to the ball. For instance on a called hit and run the runner takes off with the pitch to steal second base. The batter hits a fly to center field. The runner stops and retreats back to first.

The coach in the pitching circle helps the batter, while the coach at first checks the runner's fundamentals and whether she made the proper baserunning decision. If the coach gives the hitter no specific instructions, the hitter looks for a good pitch to hit and the base runner practices her leads, reacting to the hit if there is one. The rest of the players work on defense.

32. Feet apart, knees bent.

33. Weight evenly distributed.

Baserunning

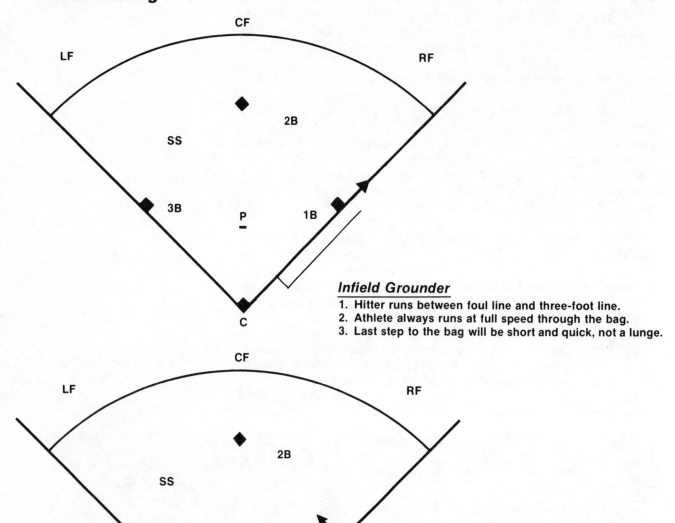

Infield Grounder
1. Hitter runs between foul line and three-foot line.
2. Athlete always runs at full speed through the bag.
3. Last step to the bag will be short and quick, not a lunge.

Single to Outfield
1. First two strides out of batter box, hitter runs directly toward first.
2. After first two strides runner begins angling out so she'll be able to arc into bags.
3. The size of the arc is different for each individual.
4. When arcing into base always hit the bag with the left foot on the inside corner.
5. Round first base hard and pick up ball, then retreat to bag, keeping eye on ball.

Baserunning, continued

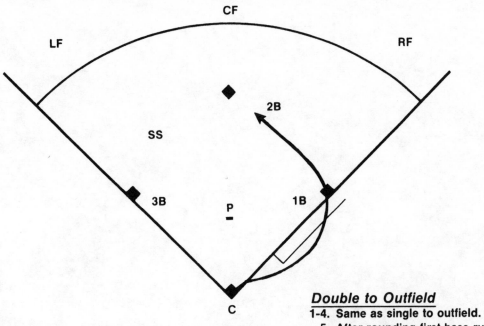

Double to Outfield
1-4. Same as single to outfield.
   5. After rounding first base run in a direct line to second.

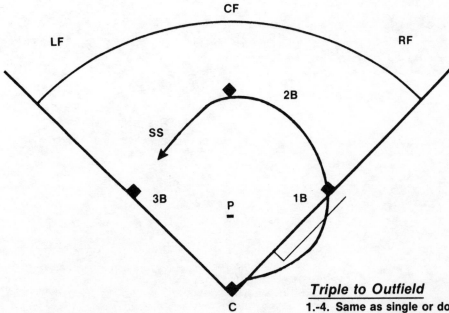

Triple to Outfield
1.-4. Same as single or double to outfield.
   5. After making contact with first base runner immediately begins to arc into second.
   6. After rounding second run in a direct line to third.

7

Sliding

All players should be taught sound, fundamental sliding skills. These skills should be developed to the extent that they may be executed correctly, safely, and without fear. Sliding is an essential skill in softball because it decreases injuries caused by sudden stops and increases the opportunity to safely advance an extra base. For all slides, run and slide at full speed. Practically speaking, by the time a runner is halfway to the bag she must decide which type of slide to execute.

Bent-Leg Slide

The bent-leg slide is preferred by many coaches over the straight-in slide because it is safer and it leads into the pop-up slide.

- Begin the slide 10-15 feet away from the bag.
- Drop the hips.
- Shoot the right leg out toward the bag and bend the left leg under the right knee to form an upside-down figure four.
- Try to glide across the top of the ground.
- Slide on the buttocks, not on the side of the hips.
- When on the ground, stay as flat as possible while keeping the head, arms, and hands off the ground. The chin should be tucked tightly to the chest to protect the head.
- The extended foot should be held 6-8 inches off the ground to prevent it from jamming into the bag.
- Slide into the bag with the extended heel moving across the top of the bag and the shin of the bent leg coming in contact with the bag.

Pop-Up Slide

This slide begins as a normal bent-leg slide. It is used in an overthrow situation and enables the runner to pop up quickly and advance to the next base.

- The pop-up slide starts the same as the bent-leg slide.
- The body is perpendicular to the bag, almost sitting up.
- The force generated by her bent left leg contacting the bag will bring the runner up.
- The runner will pop up over the bag, planting her right foot on the far side of the bag and pushing off with her left foot to the next base.
- On a pop-up slide the runner must always bend her left leg.

34-36. Bent-leg slide.

34. Begin slide 10-15 feet from bag.

35. Drop hips, keep hands high, and slide on buttocks.

36. Slide as flat as possible, tuck chin, and extended foot moves across top of bag.

Head-First Slide

The head-first slide is the fastest and most controlled slide. It is also the most dangerous. This slide should be taught, but it should be up to the runner whether or not to use it.

- As the runner approaches the bag she should drop her head and shoulders.
- Push off one leg.
- Land on the stomach, abdomen, and thighs.
- The hands and arms should be extended out toward the base.
- Bend the knees so as not to drag the feet.
- The head should be back to prevent the chin from coming in contact with the ground.
- Glide on top of the ground.
- The hands should reach for the bag, but should not be on the ground.

37-40. Head-first slide.

37. **Drop head and shoulders, arms back, and push off one leg.**

38. **Slide on stomach, abdomen, and thighs.**

39. **Extend hands and arms to base, knees bent, head back.**

40. **Hands reach for bag.**

41-43. Hook slide.

41. Begin slide 8-10 feet from bag.

42. Drop hips, throw right leg to outfield, slide with body away from tag.

43. Straighten trailing leg (left), reach to catch the bag, hands up.

Hook Slide

The hook slide is used to slide away from the ball and minimize the body area to be tagged. The explanation outlined below will be for a slide when the throw is from center or right field.

- When approaching the bag, slightly angle the running pattern toward the infield side of the bag. The runner decides on the hook slide when she realizes there will be a close play at the base.
- Begin the slide 8-10 feet away from the bag.
- In one continuous motion, plant the right leg, throw the left leg toward the infield, and drop the hips, gliding over the top of the ground.
- The trailing leg (right) is straightened out, reaching for the bag.
- Contact the bag with the top third of the right foot and continue the slide past the bag to create the hook.

Teaching Aids

- Before taking the players on the infield, water down a portion of the outfield grass and have the players practice sliding on the slick surface. Slide in tennis shoes or socks.
- A fun way to teach sliding and refresh the players is to buy or make a slip-n-slide, a plastic surface that can be covered with water, and let the athletes slide over this very slippery surface. Slide in socks or bare feet to prevent damage to the plastic.

8

Teaching the Overhand Throw

In spite of its importance as the basic throw for almost all throwing situations, the overhand throw is one of the most neglected areas when teaching softball. Without instruction, young athletes tend to either push the ball or drop their arm down to throw sidearm, thinking that if they throw the ball higher they will get more distance. Lack of arm strength in young players and lack of knowledge develop bad habits that haunt players for years, perhaps their entire careers. The overhand throw allows players to put the most velocity on the ball and throw for the most distance; therefore teaching the overhand throw should be a priority. The following is a step-by-step progression for teaching this throw.

Step forward with the right leg to begin the momentum toward the target. Bring the left foot forward while rotating the shoulders and hips and pushing the weight back on the right foot. The left shoulder should be pointing toward the target with the right arm extended back with the wrist cocked.

As the throw is executed the weight is shifted forward to the front foot. The shoulders rotate back, square to the target, allowing the right arm to come through with the hand ending down by the left knee. The back leg steps through toward the target to complete the overhand throw.

Note that as the throw is made the arm is brought straight up with a slight bend and with the elbow passing by the head just above the right ear. As the ball is released the wrist should snap down to create the proper 6-12 rotation on the ball and add greater velocity. The longer the distance, the higher the release point.

Build-Up Drills

- The fielder drops down on one knee to concentrate on the upper half of her body. First the athlete brings her arm up to its proper position by her right ear and practices the snap and follow-through to a partner about 15 feet away. Next, the fielder extends her arm back and then executes the entire motion with her arm, shoulder, and wrist.
- The fielder stands facing a fence with her shoulders square to it. In a windmill motion, she practices extension, follow-through, and snap, throwing the ball into the fence, some 15 feet away. Next, have the fielder stand sideways to the fence, her shoulder pointing at the imagined target, to work on shoulder rotation and the follow-through by her left knee. To emphasize the follow-through, ask the player to touch the grass after the throw.
- Working in partners, who are standing about 60 feet apart, players toss easy flies to each other, working on throwing mechanics and the weight shift from the back to front foot. Gradually increase the distance between the partners, working on the release point and the velocity of the throw.

44-48. Overhand throw.

44. Step with right foot.

45. Rotation.

46. Left shoulder faces target, right arm extended back.

47. Right arm brought straight up, elbow passes by ear, wrist snap, weight on front foot.

48. Right arm follows through to left knee, back leg steps toward target.

9

Infield Fundamentals

This chapter covers training the infielder. It is broken down into two sections; the first section describes general fundamentals that apply to all infielders, and the second covers skills specific to the various positions.

The Ready Position

The stance should be comfortable, somewhere between standing erect and squatting down, with the feet just about shoulder-width apart and the weight forward. The glove should be open with the pocket of the glove directed toward home plate and in front of the body. If the player has trouble keeping the glove open, she can rotate the glove outward with complete supination of the wrist.

Positioning

There is no perfect position for an infielder to stand. She must make that decision based on the hitter's tendencies and the pitcher's ability. In general, the shortstop and second baseman shade toward second base, whereas the first and third baseman are about three steps off their respective foul lines. In late innings, infielders at first and third should protect against extra-base hits by guarding the lines. The fielder must be aware of the catcher's glove position (where the pitch is to be thrown) and the type of hitter (pull or opposite field, power or singles) and adjust accordingly.

Concentration

Infielders should be aware of the outs, where the play should be if the ball is hit, and the speed of the baserunners and hitter. They must be in control at all times and talk on every play. Calling fly balls, instructing other fielders where to throw the ball, and communicating on double plays can make the difference between executing a good play and making an error because of uncertainty.

49. Ready position.

50-55. Fielding movement to left.

50. Drop step with left foot.

51. Angle.

52. Arc.

53. Move in.

54. Move in, reach for ball.

55. Field ball.

Movement

When a ball is hit to the infield, the player must position her body in front of the ball. Infielders always lead with their glove no matter which direction they move.

On balls hit directly at her, the player moves in under control, charging hard only on the slow roller. The infielder "picks her hop" or anticipates where the last hop will bring the ball before she catches it and then moves in to field the ball.

An infielder never backs up on a ground ball or a one-hop line drive. If the line drive hits about seven feet from the player or closer, she must charge and block the ball, keeping her head down, watching the ball all the way into the glove. Even if the ball is not fielded cleanly, when it is hit that hard there is plenty of time to pick it up and throw the runner out.

On balls hit away from her, the infielder should drop step at full speed and arc to align herself in the proper fielding position. This technique is accomplished in three steps: the drop step, the angle, and the arc.

In the first step the fielder opens her hips to gain depth. Her lead leg determines the proper angle for pursuing the ball while her opposite leg follows the same path. Next, she uses the angle to continue to gain depth and cover ground in pursuit of the ball. The third step starts with a deceleration of foot speed at the top of the angle, enabling the fielder to arc into the path of the ball. The top of the angle is one running stride away from the anticipated path of the ball. Until this point, the fielder should be running at full speed. The purpose of the arc is to allow the fielder to position herself in front of the ball and square her shoulders to the base that she is throwing to.

56-61. *Fielding movement to right.*

56. Drop step with right foot.

57. Angle.

58. Start arc.

59. Middle arc.

60. Finish arc.

61. Move in to field ball.

Fielding

Once the fielder has picked her hop and determined where she will field the ball, she moves into the ball by throwing out her legs farther than shoulder-width apart, enabling her to drop her hips and reach out for the ball. Her arms should be extended in front of her body with the back of her glove touching the ground. Her hips should be down, with her back almost parallel to the ground. Infielders should have soft hands, bringing the ball into their stomach, giving with the velocity of the ball, and watching it all the way into the glove.

Whenever a defensive player drops or mishandles a ball, she should pick it up barehanded. Players should never pick up the ball with their glove and then take it out with their throwing hand.

Throwing

Infielders should be taught to throw overhand. This throw is preferred because of the true rotation of the ball and the velocity it creates. Also, this throw develops habits that will be called upon on longer throws, such as relay throws to home plate. At times, other throws such as the underhand toss, snap, or sidearm throw are necessary, but the overhand throw is the basic throw to be used. The snap throw is explained in detail in the section on rundowns.

Pop-Ups

Players should move to the ball with their arms in a natural running position, getting behind the ball and then reaching up to catch it above their heads. As the ball is caught, the hands give, bringing the ball to the chest to prepare for a possible throw.

On a ball hit near a fence, the fielder must move directly to the fence, come in contact with the fence, and then retreat out to catch the ball. Once the fence is located the fielder can concentrate on fielding the ball.

62. Underhand toss.

Drills

Pickups
Two partners face each other, no more than 10 feet apart. The player with the ball tosses a grounder to the left of her partner, who stays low, moving to the ball and tossing it back to her partner. The player with the ball again tosses the ball, this time to her partner's right, where she retrieves it once again. The fielder keeps moving left and right, fielding the ball, all the while keeping her body down in the proper position. In the same basic drill, have the partners face each other across a baseline. Both players shuffle down the line toward the next base, all the while tossing the ball back and forth to each other.

Drop Steps
Players practice as partners, executing a drop step 25 times to each side, arcing, and moving in to field the ball.

Shoulder Toss
Two partners face each other, about 10 feet apart. The player with the ball tosses an easy fly over her partner's left or right shoulder. The fielder uses a drop step to get behind the ball and field it in the proper position. Never let the fielder drift backward. The first few steps to get behind the ball should be at full speed.

63. Fielding position shows back of glove on ground.

64. Fielding position shows arm extension.

Playing First Base

Accepting Throws

On a ground ball hit to the infield, the first baseman turns toward the infield and retreats to her bag. With her shoulders square to the throw, she touches the bag with her heel or heels. She is slightly crouched, with her left foot in front of her right foot and her feet spread far enough apart to keep her mobile. As the throw is made she must decide whether or not she can catch it, whether she can catch it in the air, and whether to stretch and meet the ball or to drop to the ground and block it.

If the ball cannot be caught while staying on the bag, the fielder must leave the bag to make the play. If the ball can be caught in the air, the fielder waits until the last possible second, plants her right foot on the infield side of the bag, and then stretches to meet the ball. This is accomplished in one continuous hop-step motion. As her right foot is lifted and comes back on the bag, her weight is shifted forward as she stretches with her left leg. After the stretch, the fielder comes off the bag and positions herself to throw. The most common fault is to stretch too soon, making it more difficult or impossible to catch the high throw or a throw that is off to one side. A mistake that may lead to injury occurs when the fielder places her right foot on top of or over first base.

On balls thrown to either side, the fielder moves down the bag in the direction of the throw, but continues to keep contact with the bag with her right foot. Even on throws wide to the right, the player keeps her right foot on the bag; first basemen should always use a crossover step on balls thrown to their right to get the maximal distance on the stretch.

On balls thrown to the player's left that pull her off the bag, the first baseman must catch the ball and in the same motion sweep across the line, attempting to make the tag. If the throw is high, she must leap to make the catch and then bring the glove down as soon as possible to try to tag the runner as she approaches first base.

If the ball is thrown directly at first base, but too high, the ready position will allow the defensive player to spring up for the catch. If the ball is thrown in the dirt, the first baseman must decide whether to stretch and catch it on the short hop or drop down and block the ball. The important point is to stop the ball.

Pickoffs

After the pitcher releases the ball, the first baseman breaks to the bag, opening up toward the foul line. The actual time when the player should break depends upon the speed of the pitcher and the quickness of the first baseman. Her distance from the bag also depends upon her size and quickness, but generally she is no more than 9-10 feet from the bag or 2-3 running strides. She then fields the throw on her last stride and drops the tag straight down at the side of the bag. The fielder should not be retreating too close to the foul line because she will force a throw to the outside of the bag, causing her to have to sweep across the bag to make the tag. Since the first baseman has her back to the runner, she must maintain her balance and be able to turn around quickly after attempting the tag in case the runner tries to steal second base.

The Double Play

On the hard-hit grounder to her, the first baseman should execute a jump turn, opening up toward second base. She never turns her back on the infield, but spins around, leading with her left shoulder. The only exception is when a hard grounder hit to her left forces a complete weight shift to her lead leg so that the player must fight to regain her balance before she can throw. In all cases, the throw should be on the infield side of second base.

65-68. First baseman: accept throws.

65. Touch bag with heel or toe.

66. Use a crossover step for outside throw.

67. Adjustment to inside throw.

68. Adjustment to outside throw.

Rundowns

Anytime a runner attempts to steal second, it is the first baseman's responsibility to trail that runner. This is especially important in the first and third situation, where she may be asked to make a quick tag before the runner at third can score. Further details are given in Chapter 10.

Extra-Base Hits and Cutoffs

It is the first baseman's responsibility to watch runners to make sure they touch all the bases in an extra-base hit. Whenever there is a play at the plate, the first baseman should move to the cutoff position, which is dictated by the strength of the outfielder's arm and the distance she is from home plate. The cutoff player must assume she will be cutting the ball, so she must always move her body into position, raising her arms, but only catching the ball if told to by the catcher or if the throw is way off line. The third baseman is the cutoff on all hits to left field.

Fielding Bunts

In all bunting situations and when a potential drag bunter is at the plate, the first baseman should play down the line toward home. The actual distance varies according to the field conditions, the first baseman's ability, and the speed and ability of the bunter. The player must be close enough to field a soft bunt and yet not so close that a punch (push bunt) or fake bunt gets by her. She should always move in under control.

The first baseman can either field the ball with her bare hand or sweep it into her throwing hand with her glove. When throwing to first she should open her hips toward the line so that she does not throw across her body. This also gives the second baseman a good view of the ball. On throws to second or third she should jump-turn to align her body and make the hard overhand throw.

With a runner at third and a possible suicide situation, the fielder must charge hard on the bunt and release it quickly to the catcher with an underhand toss.

69. Field ball.

69-71. First baseman: field bunt.

70. Open hips toward line.

71. Throw to first.

Playing Third Base

Pickoffs

On the release of the ball by the pitcher, the third baseman breaks to her bag, opening up toward the foul line. Her distance from the bag depends upon her size and quickness, but generally she should be no more than 9-10 feet or 2-3 running strides from the bag. On the break to the bag she leads with her glove to accept the throw. The tag may be made on the run or at third base, depending upon the circumstances. Since she has to break with her back toward the rest of the infield, she must maintain her balance so that she can come around to check the other runners after the pickoff attempt.

Cutoffs

The third baseman is the cutoff for hits to left field. Her position is dictated by her distance from home plate and the strength of the outfielder's arm. The fielder needs to align herself between the outfielder who is fielding the ball and home plate. From this point, she raises her arms to form a large target to guide the throw to the plate.

72. Cut-off stance.

73-78. Third baseman: relay to plate.

73. Catch throw from outfielder, hips open.

74. Turn, begin throw.

75. Open hips toward line.

76. Eyes on target.

77. Shoulders square to target.

78. Follow through.

Fielding Bunts

Except for the fact that the bunt play is in front of the third baseman, all the basics of positioning are the same as those detailed under the first base section. Because the third baseman has the best angle to field the ball and throw to first or second, she should be the most aggressive in fielding bunts. The third baseman must walk a tightrope between playing deep enough to handle hard shots down the line and moving up quick enough to handle sacrifice and drag bunt situations.

Accepting Throws (the tag and force play)

When accepting a throw, an infielder should sprint to the base and position herself to field the ball in the center of her body. If the ball arrives on the fly, the fielder catches the ball and then drops her glove directly to the bag. The glove should give with the force of the slide or tag to avoid a sudden collision that may jar the ball loose. This tag should be made with the glove only, because using both hands exposes the bare hand to injury. This method is used on the normal and close tag play, because when the fielder tries to bring her glove to the runner instead, the tag tends to be too high, which allows the base runner to slide under the tag.

On the forceout, the infielder must sprint to her bag as soon as possible, but she will play the ball as would a first baseman. For further explanation refer to the first base section on accepting throws.

79. Third baseman: accept throw at third base.

Playing Second Base

Pickoffs

On a pickoff at first, the second baseman decoys her positioning by moving toward the infield fringe in order to cheat closer to first and remove herself from the baserunner's vision. On the pitcher's downward swing she then breaks to the foul line, arcing to the bag. As she approaches the base, she breaks down and drops her hips in anticipation of the throw. The throw must come on the inside of first base and no higher than the knees to assure a quick and easy tag.

For a pickoff at second, the player must cheat 12-15 feet from the bag, decoying the runner much as she did for the pickoff at first. On the pitch she breaks to the front corner of the bag to accept the throw in the proper position as described earlier. If the base runner slides back to the bag, the second baseman drops down and places the tag on the ground by the base. If the runner is caught just off the bag, the second baseman starts the rundown. If the baserunner tries to advance to the next base, the fielder throws to third.

80-82. Second baseman: knee turn.

80. **Field ball.**

81. **Rotate hips toward base, drop down on knee.**

82. **Shoulders square to base, snap throw.**

The Double Play

Throws

There are three basic throws used by the second baseman in the double play: the underhand toss, the knee turn, and the jump turn. All throws should be aimed at the shortstop's chest.

When fielding a ball close to second base, an underhand toss is recommended. After catching the ball, the player steps toward the base to initiate the underhand toss. In one motion the player takes the ball out of her glove and, with her arm extended and a stiff wrist, tosses it directly to second base. The weight shift causes a natural continuation of the body toward second.

From an area midway between first and second, the second baseman uses a knee turn and a snap throw. After fielding the ball, the player rotates her hips toward second base while dropping down on her left knee. Her weight is over her hips and her shoulders are square to second base. At the same time she takes the ball out of the glove and executes a snap throw to the shortstop. This technique is accomplished in one continuous motion and starts right after fielding the ball. If properly executed, the second baseman is in perfect position for a quick snap throw to second.

On hits near first base, the player should execute a jump turn. After fielding the ball, the second baseman jumps and rotates her hips 180 degrees, ending up with her left shoulder pointing toward second base. She is now in a ready position, with her knees bent, and prepared to make the overhand throw.

Accepting Throws

There are four basic rules to remember when accepting a throw. The fielder should run to the bag at full speed in order to be there waiting for the throw. She should always square her shoulders to the throw, and she should reach out for the ball with both hands. Finally, she should catch the ball in the pocket of the glove, not the webbing.

On balls hit to the shortstop that carry her close to second but not in a position to make the play, the second baseman takes the throw off the back of the bag. With her feet shoulder-width apart, she places her left foot on the bag and keeps her right foot 1½ feet behind it. After catching the toss from the shortstop, the second baseman picks up her left foot, rocks back on her right foot, and squares her shoulders to make the throw to first.

On balls hit away from the base, the second baseman comes to the shortstop side of the bag and places her right heel against the bag. As she reaches for the throw, her left foot steps away from the base path and toward the pitcher. As the catch is made, the player shuffles off the bag into a throwing position toward first base. The step and shuffle will take the fielder away from the bag and the oncoming runner.

83-88. Second baseman: jump turns (two sequences.)

83. Field ball.

84. Jump and rotate.

85. Overhand throw.

86. Jump.

87. Rotate.

88. Overhand throw.

Bunt Situations

In all bunt situations the second baseman is responsible for covering first base. When the batter squares around, she moves toward first and comes in to fill the gap between the pitcher and the first baseman. She must maintain her position until she is sure the bunt is down and no punch or fake bunt is attempted before moving to first.

On a throw from the first baseman or catcher, the fielder moves to the proper position at first, with the side of her left foot up against the bag, preparing to receive the throw. On throws from the pitcher or third baseman, the fielder positions herself in the same manner as the first baseman accepting throws.

Relays and Tandems

The second baseman is the relay person on all hits to right field and acts as the tandem when the shortstop is the relay. Complete positioning details are given in the shortstop section.

Accepting Throws

See details under the third base section.

89-91. Second baseman: double play (throw from shortstop).

89. Position at back of bag.

90. Accept throw, then rock back.

91. Turn to throw.

92-97. *Second baseman: double play (throw from shortstop).*

92. Position in front of bag.

93. Step toward pitcher to accept throw.

94. Shuffle to throwing position.

95. Throwing position away from bag.

96. Overhand throw.

97. Follow through.

Playing Shortstop

The Double Play

Throws

Like the second baseman, the shortstop uses three basic throws in the double play: the underhand toss, the knee turn, and the throw from the hole.

The underhand toss is executed in the same manner as described earlier for the second baseman, except the shortstop uses the opposite motion and leg. In the knee turn, the action is again similar except the opposite knee goes down and the glove must be taken back out of the way. Further, the shortstop has the option to not bring her knee all the way down to the ground.

The throw for the ball hit in the hole behind third base demands the quickest release by the shortstop since it is the longest throw she has to make in the double play. In making this play, the fielder must time the catch in order to plant her right foot, field the ball, and throw to second, all in one continuous motion.

98-100. Shortstop: throw from hole behind third base.

98. Field ball.

99. Plant foot.

100. Throw.

101. Field ball.

101-103. Shortstop: knee turn.

102. Stay low, turn.

103. Hips face target, throw.

Accepting Throws

The same four basic rules apply that were listed for the second baseman. The positions vary for the shortstop based on whether the throw comes from the second baseman, the pitcher, or the first baseman.

On balls hit to the second baseman, the shortstop places her right toe near the corner of the bag, faces right field, and keeps the left foot back, preparing for the throw. As she reaches for the ball, she steps away from the base path and toward right field with her left leg. As the catch is made the shortstop drags her right leg along the side of the bag, shuffling into a throwing position. The step and shuffle will take the fielder away from the bag and the oncoming runner.

On the ball hit to the pitcher, the shortstop comes to the back corner of the bag, then executes the catch and throws in the same manner described above.

When the ball is hit to the first baseman, the shortstop yells "Inside," places her left toe on the left field corner of the bag, and prepares for the throw. As the throw comes in, she steps with her right leg toward the throw and reaches for the ball. As she catches the ball she drags her left foot over the corner of the bag and steps toward first in a throwing motion. Both steps will take her away from the bag and the runner.

Relays and Tandems

The shortstop handles all relay throws from the left and center fielders. She must position her body between the outfielder and the base she is throwing to. When a cutoff is needed, she must execute

104-107. Shortstop: double play (throw from second baseman).

104. Right toe at back corner of bag.

105. Step toward right field with left leg.

the catch and throw as quickly and accurately as possible. Also, she must be aware of the strength of the outfielder's arms and the aligment to the base where the throw is to be made.

Being able to make a smooth transition from the catch to the throw is the key to a successful relay. In making the play, the shortstop squares her shoulders to the outfielder making the play. As she catches the ball, in one continuous motion she opens her hips, turns her left shoulder to the base she must throw to, and makes the overhand throw.

The tandem is a safety valve used when a sure extra-base hit occurs. On balls hit to right field, the shortstop leaves the bag and moves to a position between the second baseman and the base where the play will be made. If an overthrow occurs, the shortstop moves to the ball and reacts to any situation that develops. The second baseman acts as the tandem when the shortstop handles the relay.

Pickoffs

When the shortstop executes a pickoff at third she uses the same principles as the second baseman does when working the pickoff at first. A pickoff attempt at second base is the same as for the second baseman, except the shortstop breaks to the left-field corner of the bag.

Accepting Throws

See details under the third base section.

106. Catch ball, drag right leg along bag.

107. Step into throwing position.

108-111. Shortstop: double play (throw from first baseman).

108. Yell "Inside".

109. Left toe on left field corner, step with right leg.

110. Catch ball, drag left foot over bag.

111. Step toward first.

10

The One-Throw Rundown

The rundown is often the most comical play in softball. Teams spend hours learning a complicated system of backups, hoping that by sheer numbers an exhausted runner will eventually tire and be tagged by one of several defensive players. Many times, however, luck stays with the runner, and an errant throw from the time-consuming game of catch finds her sitting safe on a base.

The one-throw rundown evolved from the need for a quicker and more efficient way to handle the rundown. The first rule is that the defensive player (the one with the ball) must run at the baserunner at full speed, holding the ball in clear view by her ear. The first option is to literally "run down" the baserunner. If she is unable to catch the runner, the second option involves the throw. As the first defensive player runs at the baserunner, a second infielder positions herself inside the baseline just in front of the base. As the runner is chased toward her, the second infielder accelerates toward the runner and yells "Now" when she wants the ball thrown to her.

The infielder calls for the ball when the runner is just a few feet from her. If the baserunner has been forced to run at full speed and the timing is correct between the two infielders, the second defensive player should be able to make a quick tag as the runner attempts to stop or change directions. Remember these basic principles:

- The first option is to "run down" the baserunner.
- The baserunner must be forced to retreat at full speed so that she will be unable to change directions once the ball has been thrown to the second defender.
- A snap throw must be used because it is quicker, more accurate, and reduces the chances of an overthrow.
- The second defender must accelerate toward the baserunner as she calls for the ball so that the runner will not have time to stop and change directions before the tag is made.
- Except when there is a runner on third attempting to score and the quick out is the first priority, the baserunner should be run back to the base she started from.

112. Chase runner at full speed.

Even with this technique there are times when the players will not execute the play with one throw, so a backup system must be designed to prepare for those times. If it takes more than two throws to execute the play, however, practice rundowns more often.

Backups

A very simple backup system calls for an additional player at each bag, other than the two immediately involved. Any of the infielders may be involved, including the pitcher, and depending upon the defensive alignment an outfielder may also be used. For instance, in a bunt situation with a runner on first, a left fielder covering third base may be involved should the runner try to go from first to third on the throw to first.

The movement of the first two infielders involved in the rundown is also simple. After the person with the ball (the first defender) runs at the baserunner and makes the throw to the second defender, the first defender continues running down the baseline to the next base and becomes the backup should the play return to that base. This system of movement continues as long as the rundown continues.

The outfielders, with the one exception in a bunt situation, are used as deep backups so that the ball will not advance far into the outfield if any wild throws are made. The outfielders should be lined up with the bases and about 30 feet back and should always be in a ready position.

The Snap Throw

The snap throw is used at a short distance in order to get the ball quickly and accurately to another player without overpowering her. It is executed by bringing the ball up to the ear with the arm bent. The arm is then extended, snapping the wrist down, always aiming to hit the person chest high. The arm should end up parallel to the ground,

112-116. One-throw run-down.

113. Hold ball by ear.

114. Snap throw.

with the wrist snapped and the fingers pointing toward the ground. Do not bring the arm across the body or follow through past the point that is parallel to the ground. Bringing the arm across the body will draw the ball in that direction (off line from the desired throw), and continued arm motion toward the ground will increase the chances of throwing the ball low.

The snap throw needs to be practiced often. It should be a controlled throw and yet must be executed with a strong snap to put the needed velocity on the throw.

First and Third Situations

The one-throw rundown works well for executing the first and third play. It gives the defense a quick resolution of the play to help prevent the runner at third from scoring before the third out.

With two outs many coaches will try to get their runner at first into a rundown so that the runner at third has time to score. With the one-throw method the runner at first is forced to run at full speed while the defender is moving down the line toward her, cutting down the distance involved. The quick tag should be made before the runner has traveled 60 feet—the distance from third to home. Under this system, the runner at third should not have time to get across home before the tag is made for the third out.

Teaching the Rundown

Teach the rundown by breaking it into four separate drills. In the first part teach the snap throw, which should be practiced every day as the players warm up. Start working on the throw while playing catch and then progress to throwing on the run.

Next, organize a partner chase between two bases. One player holds the ball while her player acts as a baserunner, starting a few steps ahead of her in the baseline. On call the baserunner takes off

115. Catch ball, accelerate toward runner.

116. Tag.

for the next base, with the defender in pursuit. This phase is concerned with the defender's initial acceleration after the runner. It also teaches the infielder how to hold the ball as she runs.

The third step is to practice calling for the ball. Again in partners, have the player with the ball run hard down the baseline toward her partner. The second defender starts moving down the line toward her partner and then calls for the ball by yelling "Now." Accurate timing between these two people is important to the rundown.

The final phase brings in a third person to act as the baserunner for the two defenders. Put all the skills together with the final emphasis on the tag. Don't progress to this stage until the players have mastered the leadup skills. As a safety precaution have the baserunners wear batting helmets.

117-120. The snap throw.

117. Arm bent. Bring ball to ear.

118. Start motion forward.

119. Extend arm, snap wrist down while releasing ball.

120. Arm follows through parallel to ground.

11

Outfield Fundamentals

This chapter deals with the specific responsibilities and skills of the outfielder. Playing the outfield takes a great deal of discipline and concentration because it is easy to let the mind drift or coast through drills unless constantly reminded of the proper fundamentals.

The Ready Position

In the ready position the outfielder should stand with her knees slightly bent, her feet square and facing home plate, her weight on the balls of her feet, and her glove held waist high. Never, in practice or game, should an outfielder be allowed to stand flatfooted with her glove and free hand resting on her knees. Outfielders must assume that every ball will be hit to them and get the best possible jump on the ball. An outfielder should never overplay the ball to the right or left.

Positioning

The player should start with a general position in the outfield, then adjust to the hitter. The outfielder should know each hitter and the ability of her own pitcher so that she can play accordingly. With a right-handed hitter, unless she is known to have power to the opposite field, the right fielder should play closer to the infield than the center or left fielder. The same logic applies to the left fielder with a left-handed hitter. In addition, the outfielder must be prepared to back up the proper bases when the hit is away from her. For instance, with no runners on base and a hit to the third baseman, the right fielder must back up first base on the throw, staying far enough back to stop a wild throw. Further, the outfielder must have the confidence to play as close as possible while still handling the power hits.

Concentration

Because an outfielder may go through several innings without having a ball hit to her, she must work hard to maintain her concentration. She should know the outs, where the play will be if the ball is hit to her, the speed of the baserunners, the score, and the backup responsibilities. There should be constant communication among the outfielders and between the outfielders and infielders regarding outs and positioning; this instills confidence and minimizes errors.

Initial Movement

One of the most common errors is for an outfielder to take a step forward or back the instant the ball is hit. Players should hold their position for a count until they know whether the ball is hit in front of them or over their head. A step in the wrong direction is much worse than that split second when the trained outfielder makes the proper judgment. Once the decision is made the fielder should get to the ball as soon as possible. Outfielders should also run on their toes in order to avoid excessive head movement.

Getting Back on the Ball

The outfielder should get back at full speed, when a ball is hit over her head, getting behind the ball is possible and fielding it in the best position to make the throw to the infield. An outfielder should never drift or time a catch. By drifting back on a ball the player invites an error and increases the chances of baserunners tagging and advancing to the next base.

Surrounding the Ball

On the average fly ball the outfielder should surround (arc) the ball to catch it on the throwing-arm side while squaring her shoulders to the base she is throwing to. When making the catch the left foot should be slightly in front of the right, and when possible the player should be behind the ball so that she can move in as she catches the ball.

121-127. Surround the ball.

121. Drop step.

122. Angle.

123. Angle.

124. Arc.

125. Arc.

126. Make the catch.

127. Prepare to throw.

Angle of Pursuit

On all balls hit away from the outfielder where there is a posibility that the ball could get by the player, the outfielder should take a drop step and pursue the ball at a hard angle to cut off the ball. The player should always run at full speed and never cut directly across to the ball.

Catching the Fly Ball

The outfielder must position herself behind the ball and maintain eye contact with it at all times. The hands stay at the sides of the body until the initial movement to field the ball. When catching the ball, both hands move to above and in front of the head, with the arms fully extended. As the catch is made the arms absorb the impact of the ball, by bringing the glove and the ball to the chest.

128. Catch fly ball above and in front of head.

Throwing

Outfielders should always throw the ball overhand. The arm extension creates more velocity and distance. Also, because of the rotation put on the ball, there will be a truer, more direct flight of the ball. On throws to the infielders, the outfielder should aim for the infielder's upper body, but on throws to the bases any throw from the waist to the ankles is acceptable as long as it can be fielded easily and is thrown to the area where the tag must be made. On long throws, the players should throw a low line drive since it is the quickest throw and can be cut off by an infielder if necessary.

The Crow Hop

The crow hop helps the outfielder throw for longer distances by using her body as well as her arm. As the fielder catches the ball she steps forward with her right leg. She then skips on her right foot, rotating her shoulders so that her left shoulder is pointed toward the target, and while maintaining her weight on her back leg, she extends her right arm back. As she executes the throw, shifting her weight forward to her front foot, her shoulders rotate back, square to the target, allowing her right arm to come through with her hand ending down by her left knee as her back leg steps through toward the target. The longer the distances, the higher the release point must be. The steps should always be in the direction of the target.

129. Move in.

129-135. The crow hop.

130. Raise glove to ball.

131. Catch ball.

132. Step forward.

133. Skip and prepare to throw.

134. Overhand throw.

135. Follow through.

Fielding the Grounder

Outfielders should field average ground balls as an infielder would. If there is a chance that the ball might get by the outfielder, she should drop down on one knee and use her other leg and her body to block the ball. If a quick throw is required, the outfielder should scoop up the ball just in front and to the left of her left foot while still on the run, bringing the ball up and executing the crow hop. The player should bring her head down to the ball, keeping the back of her glove on the ground as she fields the ball instead of trying to pick up the ball with just the tip of her glove.

Fielding Fly Balls in the Sun

When a fly ball goes into the sun, the fielder should turn her body at an angle to the sun so that she will be looking to the side and not directly into the sun. When the ball comes out of the sun she will see a shadow and react to that. In some cases the glove can be used to shield the sun and prevent the fielder from being blinded.

Playing the Wind

Fielders should always know from which direction the wind is blowing and how strong it is. If the wind is strong, players must learn to stand into the wind so that the ball will be blown to them, not away from them. Handling wind conditions is another reason the fielder must get to a fly ball as soon as possible.

136. Block grounders with your body.

137. Alternative method to block ball which leads to quicker throw.

Backing Up

Outfielders should always assume that the infielders will miss every ball that is hit to them. When the ball is not hit in an outfielder's area, she should be moving to the proper backup position. The right fielder is responsible for infielder's throws to first and for throws to second from left field. The left fielder backs up throws to third, covers third in bunt situations with a runner on first, and backs up second on throws from right field. The center fielder is primarily responsible for second base and must be quick to align herself depending upon where the throw originates. Again, outfielders should assume there will be a throwing error and get to their backup positions at full speed and at least 30 feet behind the base to guarantee that the wild throw will not get by them.

When fences are close to first and third base, the left and right fielders must know how to play the ball. The players should anticipate the angle and speed at which the ball will rebound off the fence.

Drills

Shoulder Toss

An outfielder stands in a ready position, facing a coach, who is about 10 feet away. The coach tosses a ball over one of the player's shoulders, high enough to give her time to get back of the ball and catch it in the proper position over the throwing shoulder. In the beginning the coach may tell the player where the ball will be thrown. This drill teaches the players to execute a hard drop step and to get back as quickly as possible.

138-144. Do-or-die.

138. Move in.

139. Move in.

140. Scoop up ball, back of glove on ground.

141. Prepare for throw.

142. Crow hop.

143. Overhand throw.

144. Follow through.

Point and Throw

This drill is used to teach players to get back hard and use the drop step while changing directions. An outfielder stands in a ready position, facing the coach, who is about 10 feet away. The coach yells "Go" and points to her left. The outfielder must react in that direction, executing a drop step while watching the coach over her shoulder. After a few steps, the coach points in the opposite direction so that the player will have to open up her hips and drop step to the left, all at full speed. The coach may start the drill pointing to the left or right and may make the athlete change directions as often as she wishes, but on the final drop step the coach throws a ball for the outfielder to catch.

The Blind Toss

An outfielder stands about 20 feet away from the coach with her back turned. When the coach tosses a ball in the air, she yells "Ball," at which time the player turns, locates the ball, and reacts accordingly. This teaches players to locate the ball quickly before making any moves.

Angle of Pursuit

Have all the outfielders stand in a line in center field, facing home plate. The coach hits balls to the players' left and right, making sure the proper angle of pursuit is taken.

Fly Balls

Every day, or at least three times a week, outfielders should be hit a variety of fly balls. The proper fundamentals should be emphasized with each hit. Never let a player casually catch a ball or drift as she moves to a ball. There should always be a purpose to practice.

145. Proper fundamentals should always be emphasized.

Defensive Alignment

This chapter deals with a team's defensive alignment against various offensive situations. Through a series of diagrams, it depicts the movement of the defensive players based on the location of the hit and the number of baserunners. The symbols are self-explanatory.

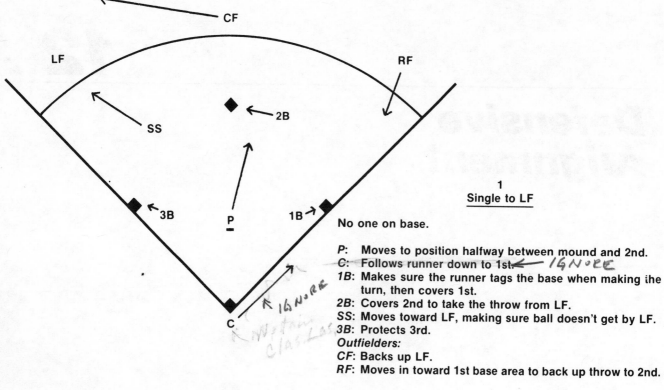

1
Single to LF

No one on base.

P: Moves to position halfway between mound and 2nd.
C: Follows runner down to 1st.← IGNORE
1B: Makes sure the runner tags the base when making the turn, then covers 1st.
2B: Covers 2nd to take the throw from LF.
SS: Moves toward LF, making sure ball doesn't get by LF.
3B: Protects 3rd.
Outfielders:
CF: Backs up LF.
RF: Moves in toward 1st base area to back up throw to 2nd.

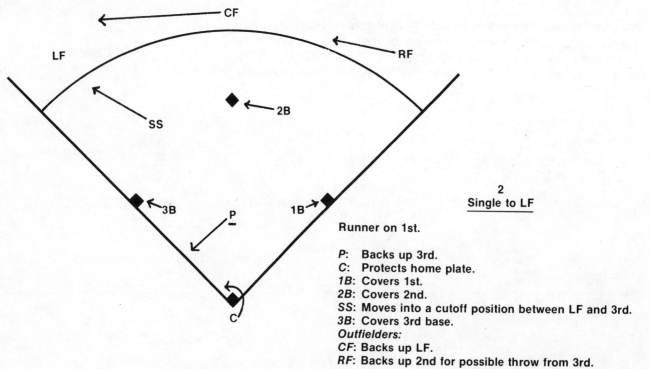

2
Single to LF

Runner on 1st.

P: Backs up 3rd.
C: Protects home plate.
1B: Covers 1st.
2B: Covers 2nd.
SS: Moves into a cutoff position between LF and 3rd.
3B: Covers 3rd base.
Outfielders:
CF: Backs up LF.
RF: Backs up 2nd for possible throw from 3rd.

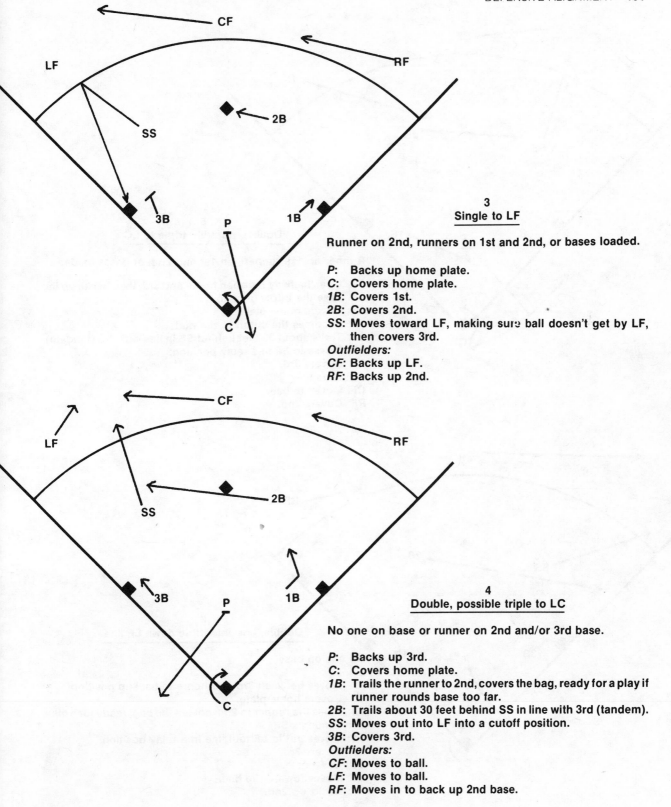

3
Single to LF

Runner on 2nd, runners on 1st and 2nd, or bases loaded.

P: Backs up home plate.
C: Covers home plate.
1B: Covers 1st.
2B: Covers 2nd.
SS: Moves toward LF, making sure ball doesn't get by LF,
      then covers 3rd.
Outfielders:
CF: Backs up LF.
RF: Backs up 2nd.

4
Double, possible triple to LC

No one on base or runner on 2nd and/or 3rd base.

P: Backs up 3rd.
C: Covers home plate.
1B: Trails the runner to 2nd, covers the bag, ready for a play if
      runner rounds base too far.
2B: Trails about 30 feet behind SS in line with 3rd (tandem).
SS: Moves out into LF into a cutoff position.
3B: Covers 3rd.
Outfielders:
CF: Moves to ball.
LF: Moves to ball.
RF: Moves in to back up 2nd base.

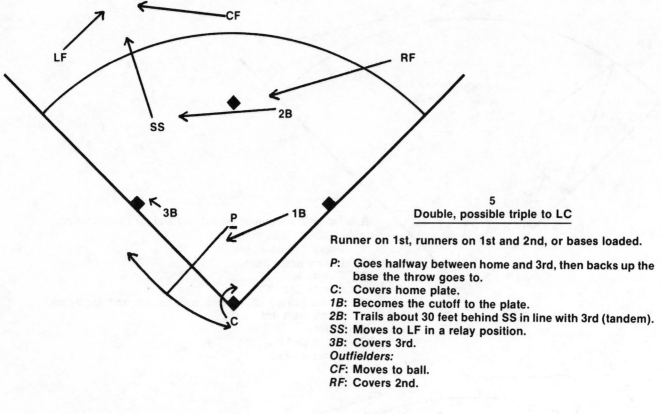

5
Double, possible triple to LC

Runner on 1st, runners on 1st and 2nd, or bases loaded.

P: Goes halfway between home and 3rd, then backs up the base the throw goes to.
C: Covers home plate.
1B: Becomes the cutoff to the plate.
2B: Trails about 30 feet behind SS in line with 3rd (tandem).
SS: Moves to LF in a relay position.
3B: Covers 3rd.
Outfielders:
CF: Moves to ball.
RF: Covers 2nd.

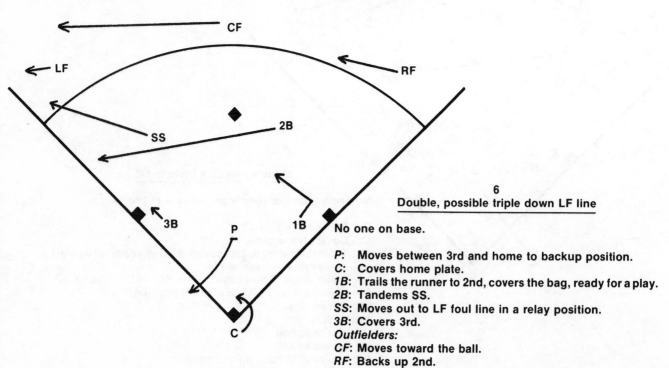

6
Double, possible triple down LF line

No one on base.

P: Moves between 3rd and home to backup position.
C: Covers home plate.
1B: Trails the runner to 2nd, covers the bag, ready for a play.
2B: Tandems SS.
SS: Moves out to LF foul line in a relay position.
3B: Covers 3rd.
Outfielders:
CF: Moves toward the ball.
RF: Backs up 2nd.

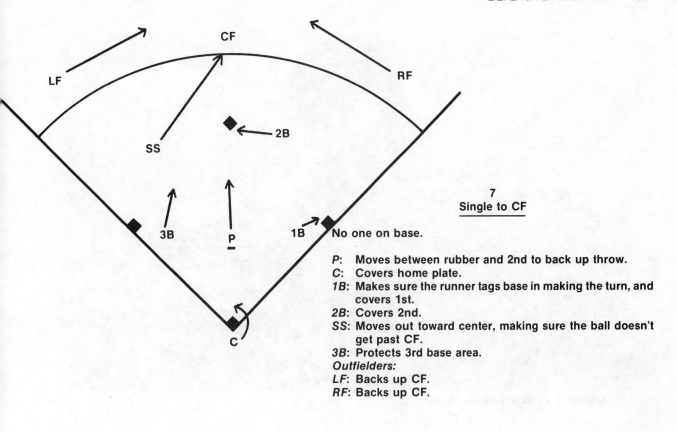

7
Single to CF

No one on base.

P: Moves between rubber and 2nd to back up throw.
C: Covers home plate.
1B: Makes sure the runner tags base in making the turn, and covers 1st.
2B: Covers 2nd.
SS: Moves out toward center, making sure the ball doesn't get past CF.
3B: Protects 3rd base area.
Outfielders:
LF: Backs up CF.
RF: Backs up CF.

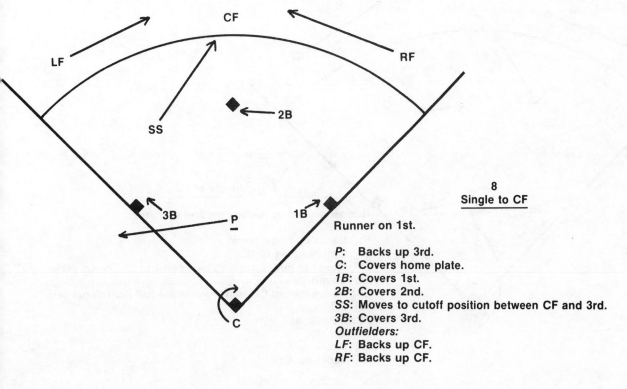

8
Single to CF

Runner on 1st.

P: Backs up 3rd.
C: Covers home plate.
1B: Covers 1st.
2B: Covers 2nd.
SS: Moves to cutoff position between CF and 3rd.
3B: Covers 3rd.
Outfielders:
LF: Backs up CF.
RF: Backs up CF.

146. The pitcher is a primary defensive player.

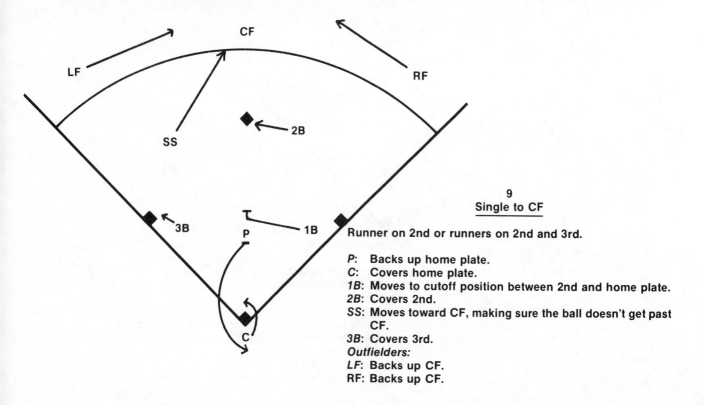

9
Single to CF

Runner on 2nd or runners on 2nd and 3rd.

P: **Backs up home plate.**
C: **Covers home plate.**
1B: **Moves to cutoff position between 2nd and home plate.**
2B: **Covers 2nd.**
SS: **Moves toward CF, making sure the ball doesn't get past CF.**
3B: **Covers 3rd.**
Outfielders:
LF: **Backs up CF.**
RF: **Backs up CF.**

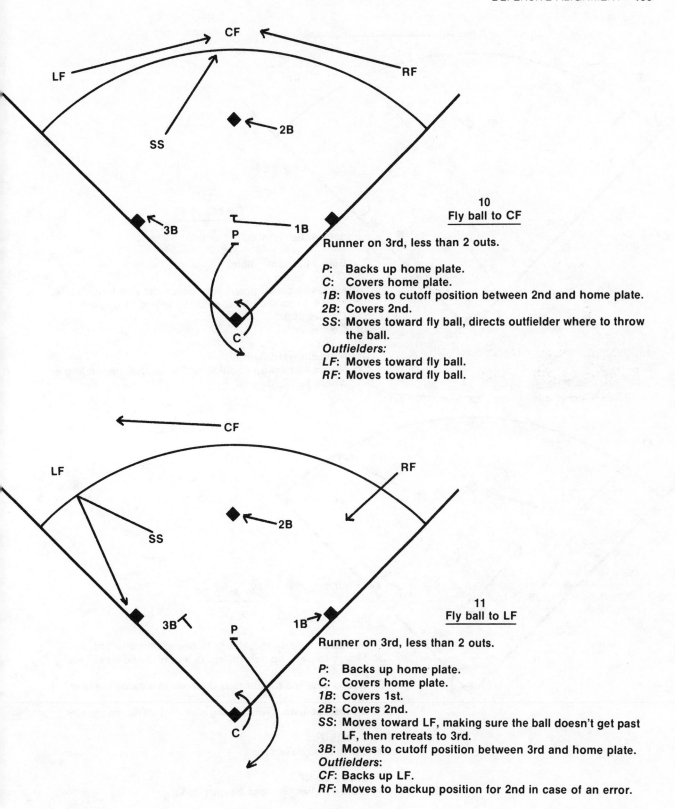

**10
Fly ball to CF**

Runner on 3rd, less than 2 outs.

P: Backs up home plate.
C: Covers home plate.
1B: Moves to cutoff position between 2nd and home plate.
2B: Covers 2nd.
SS: Moves toward fly ball, directs outfielder where to throw the ball.
Outfielders:
LF: Moves toward fly ball.
RF: Moves toward fly ball.

**11
Fly ball to LF**

Runner on 3rd, less than 2 outs.

P: Backs up home plate.
C: Covers home plate.
1B: Covers 1st.
2B: Covers 2nd.
SS: Moves toward LF, making sure the ball doesn't get past LF, then retreats to 3rd.
3B: Moves to cutoff position between 3rd and home plate.
Outfielders:
CF: Backs up LF.
RF: Moves to backup position for 2nd in case of an error.

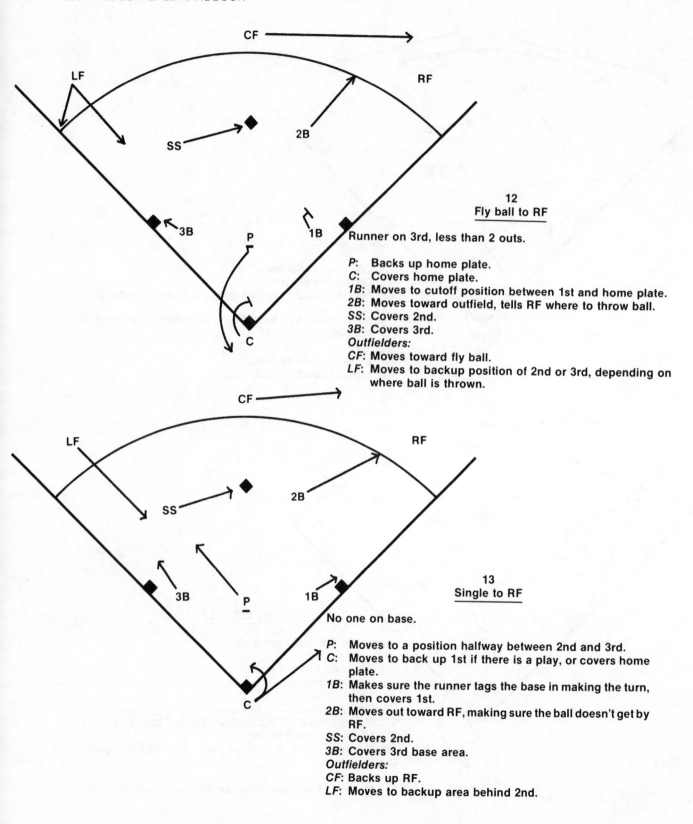

12
Fly ball to RF

Runner on 3rd, less than 2 outs.

P: Backs up home plate.
C: Covers home plate.
1B: Moves to cutoff position between 1st and home plate.
2B: Moves toward outfield, tells RF where to throw ball.
SS: Covers 2nd.
3B: Covers 3rd.
Outfielders:
CF: Moves toward fly ball.
LF: Moves to backup position of 2nd or 3rd, depending on where ball is thrown.

13
Single to RF

No one on base.

P: Moves to a position halfway between 2nd and 3rd.
C: Moves to back up 1st if there is a play, or covers home plate.
1B: Makes sure the runner tags the base in making the turn, then covers 1st.
2B: Moves out toward RF, making sure the ball doesn't get by RF.
SS: Covers 2nd.
3B: Covers 3rd base area.
Outfielders:
CF: Backs up RF.
LF: Moves to backup area behind 2nd.

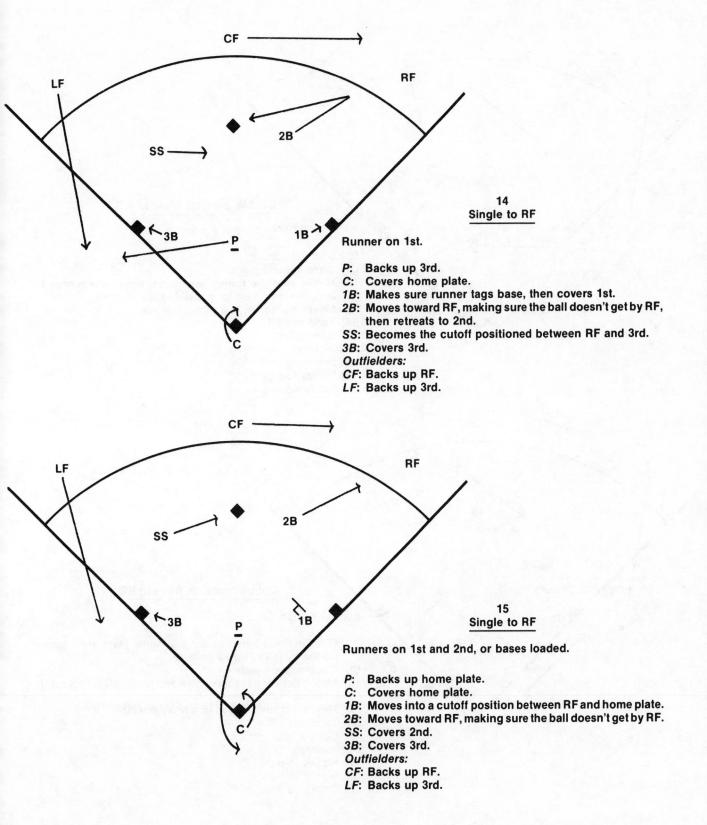

14
Single to RF

Runner on 1st.

P: Backs up 3rd.
C: Covers home plate.
1B: Makes sure runner tags base, then covers 1st.
2B: Moves toward RF, making sure the ball doesn't get by RF, then retreats to 2nd.
SS: Becomes the cutoff positioned between RF and 3rd.
3B: Covers 3rd.
Outfielders:
CF: Backs up RF.
LF: Backs up 3rd.

15
Single to RF

Runners on 1st and 2nd, or bases loaded.

P: Backs up home plate.
C: Covers home plate.
1B: Moves into a cutoff position between RF and home plate.
2B: Moves toward RF, making sure the ball doesn't get by RF.
SS: Covers 2nd.
3B: Covers 3rd.
Outfielders:
CF: Backs up RF.
LF: Backs up 3rd.

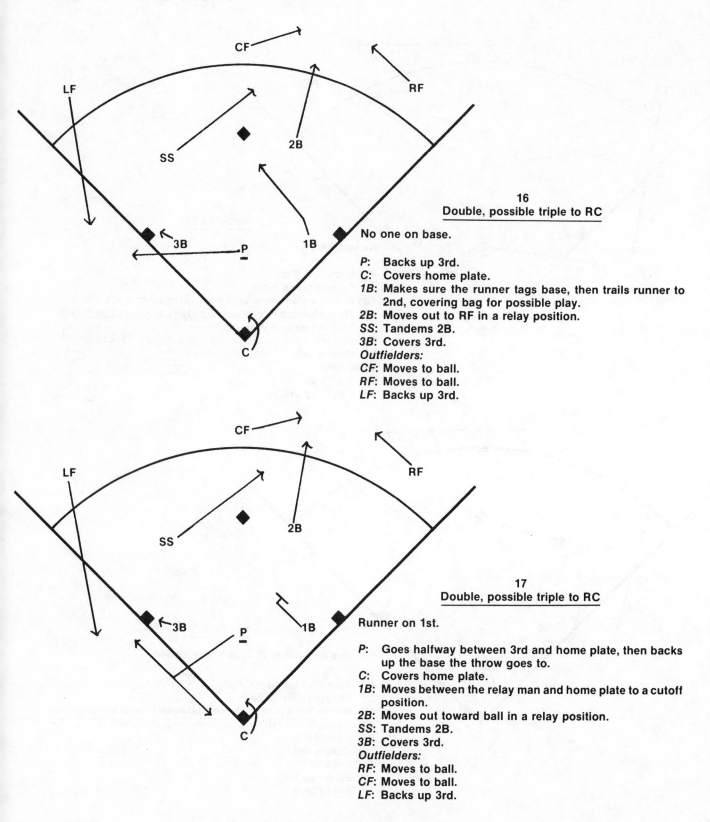

16
Double, possible triple to RC

No one on base.

P: Backs up 3rd.
C: Covers home plate.
1B: Makes sure the runner tags base, then trails runner to 2nd, covering bag for possible play.
2B: Moves out to RF in a relay position.
SS: Tandems 2B.
3B: Covers 3rd.
Outfielders:
CF: Moves to ball.
RF: Moves to ball.
LF: Backs up 3rd.

17
Double, possible triple to RC

Runner on 1st.

P: Goes halfway between 3rd and home plate, then backs up the base the throw goes to.
C: Covers home plate.
1B: Moves between the relay man and home plate to a cutoff position.
2B: Moves out toward ball in a relay position.
SS: Tandems 2B.
3B: Covers 3rd.
Outfielders:
RF: Moves to ball.
CF: Moves to ball.
LF: Backs up 3rd.

147. Outfielders must always be alert.

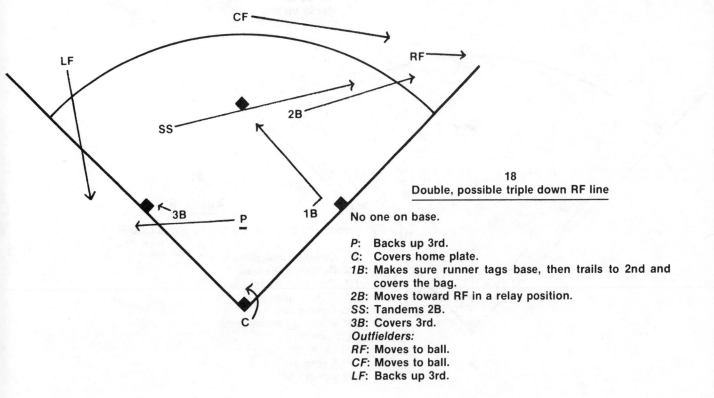

18
Double, possible triple down RF line

No one on base.

P: Backs up 3rd.
C: Covers home plate.
1B: Makes sure runner tags base, then trails to 2nd and covers the bag.
2B: Moves toward RF in a relay position.
SS: Tandems 2B.
3B: Covers 3rd.
Outfielders:
RF: Moves to ball.
CF: Moves to ball.
LF: Backs up 3rd.

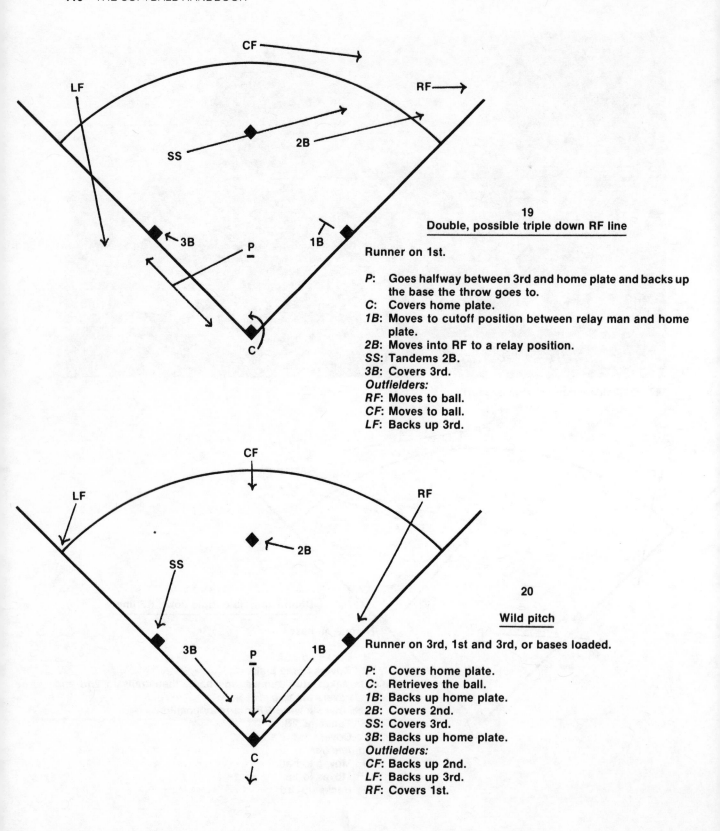

19
Double, possible triple down RF line

Runner on 1st.

P: Goes halfway between 3rd and home plate and backs up the base the throw goes to.
C: Covers home plate.
1B: Moves to cutoff position between relay man and home plate.
2B: Moves into RF to a relay position.
SS: Tandems 2B.
3B: Covers 3rd.
Outfielders:
RF: Moves to ball.
CF: Moves to ball.
LF: Backs up 3rd.

20
Wild pitch

Runner on 3rd, 1st and 3rd, or bases loaded.

P: Covers home plate.
C: Retrieves the ball.
1B: Backs up home plate.
2B: Covers 2nd.
SS: Covers 3rd.
3B: Backs up home plate.
Outfielders:
CF: Backs up 2nd.
LF: Backs up 3rd.
RF: Covers 1st.

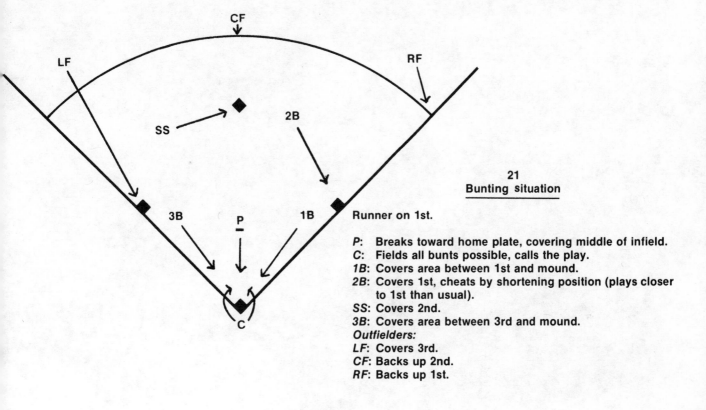

21
Bunting situation

Runner on 1st.

P: Breaks toward home plate, covering middle of infield.
C: Fields all bunts possible, calls the play.
1B: Covers area between 1st and mound.
2B: Covers 1st, cheats by shortening position (plays closer to 1st than usual).
SS: Covers 2nd.
3B: Covers area between 3rd and mound.
Outfielders:
LF: Covers 3rd.
CF: Backs up 2nd.
RF: Backs up 1st.

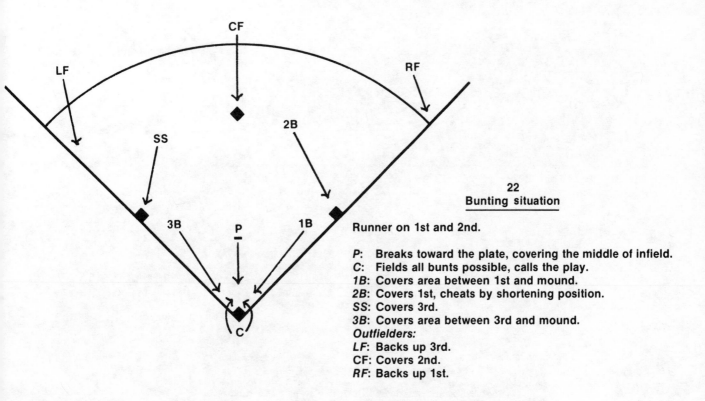

22
Bunting situation

Runner on 1st and 2nd.

P: Breaks toward the plate, covering the middle of infield.
C: Fields all bunts possible, calls the play.
1B: Covers area between 1st and mound.
2B: Covers 1st, cheats by shortening position.
SS: Covers 3rd.
3B: Covers area between 3rd and mound.
Outfielders:
LF: Backs up 3rd.
CF: Covers 2nd.
RF: Backs up 1st.

Training the Catcher

Catching has always been considered the toughest position because of the physical abuse involved. The responsibilities are many. The catcher must be strong enough to block pitches thrown in the dirt, cover the plate against sprinting baserunners, throw out stealing baserunners, handle pitchers, and decide on the strategy to be used against the hitters. As for every skill, fundamentals are the foundation; no matter how talented the athlete, there are no short cuts to mastering the skills of a quality catcher.

Position Behind the Plate
The catcher should sit up as close to home plate as possible without interfering with the batter's swing. In this position the ball is caught earlier, thereby increasing the likelihood of a strike being called. The catcher's position behind the plate is determined by the position of the batter in the batter's box.

Signals

When giving signals the catcher should squat behind the plate with her knees apart. Her glove hand should be placed outside her left knee, covering the space between her left knee and the ground. Her free hand should be placed on the inside of her right thigh, using different finger combinations to signal pitches. When signals are given the fingers should be spread far enough apart for the pitcher to read the signs easily.

The placement of the glove hand is designed to keep the third base coach from picking up the catcher's signals. The free hand is positioned to block the signals from the first base coach. If the catcher feels the runner at second base is stealing the signs, a different pattern should be used to prevent the signs from being stolen.

Down Position

This is a comfortable position for the catcher. It is used only when the bases are empty. The catcher squats down behind home plate, with her weight on the balls of her feet. Her glove hand should be extended away from her body, thereby showing the pitcher an open glove and a large target. To further increase the size of the target, align the glove with the center of the body. Protect the free hand from tipped balls by positioning it behind the back or legs.

Up Position

The up position is used when there are runners on base. This position allows the catcher to shift or execute a throw quickly and easily. The

148. Signal position.

149. Down position.

catcher is positioned with her feet shoulder-width apart and her left foot slightly in front of her right. Her back should remain parallel to the ground, with her hips held high. It is important not to drag the hips. Her glove hand should be extended away from her body, providing a large target. Her free hand should be kept behind her back or leg for protection from tipped balls.

The Target

When giving a target always hold the glove away from the body, with the extended arm just slightly bent. Spread the fingers so that the glove is open, and always keep the glove in the center of the body.

For the outside pitch the center of the body should be aligned with the outside corner of the plate. For the inside pitch align the center of the body with the inside corner of the plate. On the low pitch bring the head and shoulders down lower to the ground. For the high pitch straighten the back and extend the left arm up to the area where the ball will be pitched. Keep the glove in front of the vertical plane of the body so that the ball can be seen as it enters the glove.

Throwing Out Base Runners

When a base runner is stealing second, the catcher should lean into the ball just before catching it. As the ball is caught she executes a jump turn, rotating her shoulders parallel to the batter's box. Her glove hand is brought to her ear, meeting her throwing hand. She executes the throw by transferring weight from her back right leg to her front left leg, rotating her shoulders, and following through. Her right hand comes to her knee while her back leg steps through toward second base.

no step (right foot)

150. Up position.

With a runner attempting to steal third, on an inside pitch the catcher executes a shuffle step behind the right-handed hitter and throws the ball to third. On an outside pitch with a right-handed hitter, the catcher should step toward the pitcher's mound, with her right leg moving in front of the hitter, clearing a path for the throw. Execute the throw as usual. For any pitch with a left-handed hitter, the catcher should step toward third with her left leg and execute the throw.

The Pitchout
The pitchout is used when the catcher believes the baserunner is taking too large a lead or is trying to steal a base. The catcher calls for the pitchout and lines up on the outside edge of the plate. As the pitcher releases the ball, the catcher slides to a position outside the batter's box to field the pitch. This puts the catcher in a position to throw to any base.

Receiving Throws for a Force Play
The catcher should move in front of the plate and square her shoulders to the ball. Her right foot should be on the plate so that she can stretch to the ball in the same manner as the first baseman, catching the ball off her left leg.

Receiving Throws for a Tag Play
After the ball is hit the catcher should move in front of the plate, squaring her shoulders to face the throw. Her left foot should be placed on the front left corner of home plate. No matter where the throw comes from, the catcher should drop her hips lower than the ball to make sure she catches the ball.

151-154. Pitchout.

151. Hold glove away from body.

152. Line up on outside edge of plate.

On a close play, the catcher should catch the ball, then drop her left knee to the ground and block the plate with her shin guard. The ball should be held in her glove with her free hand around it. After the tag is made, if there is less than two outs, the catcher should immediately come up from the tag and check the other base runners. If the play is not close when the catcher receives the ball, she should move up the baseline to make the tag.

Fielding Bunts and Topped Balls

The catcher should always be responsible for fielding all balls hit in the immediate area around home plate. The catcher should circle around the ball, pointing her left shoulder toward the appropriate base. She should pick up the ball with her bare hand and execute the throw. If the runner is in the line of the throw, the catcher should step to the side and then throw.

Shifting and Blocking

When a pitch is thrown into the dirt, the catcher should concentrate on blocking the ball and keeping it in front of her body. Keeping the ball in front of her freezes the runners on base, whereas a passed ball allows the runners to advance. The catcher should always be in the up position with runners on base, but need not block and shift when there are no runners on base.

153. Field pitch outside batter's box.

154. Ready to throw.

155. Block in front.

When a ball is thrown in the dirt to the catcher's right, she should step out with the right leg keeping the pitch in the center of the body. She should then drag her left leg behind while the glove moves to between the legs, thus completing the block. When fielding the ball, the back side of the glove should be on the ground. The same principles apply to pitches thrown to the left side.

When a pitch is thrown in the dirt just in front of the catcher, she should shoot both knees out and apart, sliding into the ball on the inside of the knees. With the back side of the glove on the ground the catcher should place the glove between the legs to execute the block. The back should be bowed and the chin brought to the chest to protect the throat area and help keep the eyes on the ball.

Backing Up First Base

When there are no runners on base and a ground ball is hit to the infield, the catcher should move down the first base line to a backup position between first base and the fence. With runners on base, the catcher should stay at home plate.

156. Block to left.

157. Block to right.

Catching Pop-Ups

After the ball comes off the bat, the catcher should turn to her strong side and immediately find the ball. As she is turning she removes her mask and holds it in her free hand. Once the ball is located she should throw her mask in the opposite direction. She then should move to the ball and catch it over her head.

On a ball that is popped up to the infield side of home plate, the catcher should turn her back to the infield to adjust to the spin on the ball. On pop-ups that come close to the fence, the catcher should move to the fence quickly and then come off from the fence to make the catch.

158. Block plate with shin guard on a tag play.

1
@ top
of
windmill,
ball is
facing out
towards
3rd base

14

Training the Pitcher

There are as many pitching coaches as there are pitchers in this country. It seems that many who have pitched or have even seen a pitcher throw feel qualified to teach this difficult skill. Three highly respected instructors in the game today are Herb Dudley of Florida (who coached Darlene Lowery, now pitching for South Carolina), Bob Wright of Iowa (who coached Michelle Thomas, of the Sun City Saints), and Ron LeFebvre of California (who has developed many college pitchers, including his own daughter Susan—now pitching for Cal State, Fullerton—and Allison Maney, who pitches for the University of New Mexico).

The following fundamentals are based on the teachings of LeFebvre, the unofficial pitching coach of the University of New Mexico. These principles are the basics for coaching pitchers. Before teaching various pitches such as the drop and rise, have a qualified instructor, such as the three listed, analyze the pitcher to define the proper steps suited for that individual. The following fundamentals are based on throwing the fastball.

Fingers and the Grip

The ball is held by the fingers, not in the hand. Spin is created as the fingers apply pressure against the seams and as the wrist snaps. The grip is firm but not tight. Squeezing the ball too hard will tighten up the muscles in the hand, wrist, and forearm. Either a two-finger grip, which makes the ball float more, or a three-finger grip can be used.

Wrist Snap

A strong wrist snap is crucial to creating speed and movement on the ball. The pitcher must cock her wrist on the downward swing and snap it at the power point by her hip. This point, which varies for each individual, refers to the spot between the wrist and the hip where the perfectly timed snap results in the maximal force on the ball. On the fastball, the snap and follow-through point directly at home plate, with the first and second fingers the last to come off the ball.

The Arm

The arm acts like a whip and should be relaxed throughout the motion. A pitcher needs maximal acceleration on the downward swing with complete arm extension for leverage and rotation in a smooth plane parallel to her body.

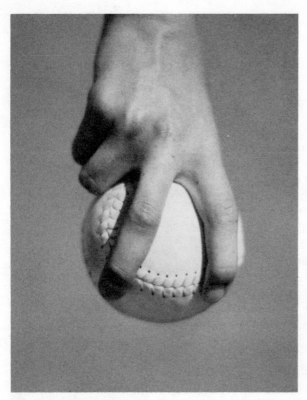

159. Two-finger grip.

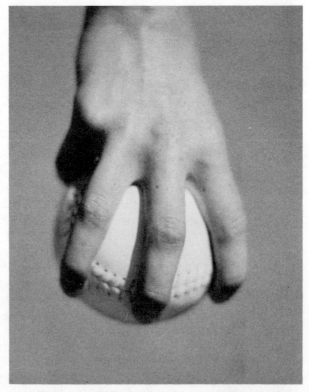

160. Three-finger grip.

The Shoulder

No pitch is made with the shoulder. The shoulders move naturally as the hips rotate, following the actions of the arm and hand, not leading them. The pitcher should never use her right shoulder to lead the action toward home or attempt to create action on the ball with her shoulder instead of her hand. As in hitting, the left shoulder should not spin out prematurely, but should open along with the hips to prepare for the arm and then close as a natural finish of the pitch.

The Hips

The hips act as a coil, storing power to be unleashed just as the hand hits the power point. The hips rotate toward third to allow the hand smooth passage by the body. If the hips square to home plate too soon, the hand must come around the hips, restricting the ability to snap and eliminating the possibility of finding the power point.

161. Power point, wrist cocked.

cocks automatically if
pitcher has ball facing 3rd base
at top of windmill.

The Left Foot

The stride of the left foot should be thought of as a step, not as a falling action. It is a controlled movement, not a fall resulting from a premature weight shift forward. The step should be straight toward home plate, with the foot landing at no more than a 45-degree angle to home. The stride is about 4½ steps of the pitcher's own foot. In the delivery, the left foot makes contact with the ground just before the ball is snapped.

162-165. Fast pitch.

162. **Approaching balance point.**

163. **Downward swing.**

164. **Approaching power point and final push to plate.**

165. **Left foot turned not more than 45°.**

Note that ball and palm of pitching hand is facing 3rd base. This will cause the pitcher to cock the wrist for the Release of the ball.

Read this page 1st

Weight Shift and Balance Point

The weight must be kept back until that explosive moment when the ball is snapped and all the power sources are thrust forward. The balance point is where the right hand is at its highest point above the head and the left foot is at its highest above the ground. At this position in the delivery, the weight is over the right heel, poised and ready for the downward swing and thrust toward home plate.

Failure to achieve the balance point means the weight has been thrown forward too early, forcing the pitcher's body (instead of her hand) to lead the pitch. With her weight and body forward, the pitcher ends up throwing with her arm alone. Trying to generate power or speed too early in the delivery often leads to this problem.

The Right Knee

The right knee bends out toward third base as the body is preparing for the balance point. This allows the body to push the hips through and opens up the shoulders and hips.

bend of right knee towards 3rd base allows hips to open up.

45°

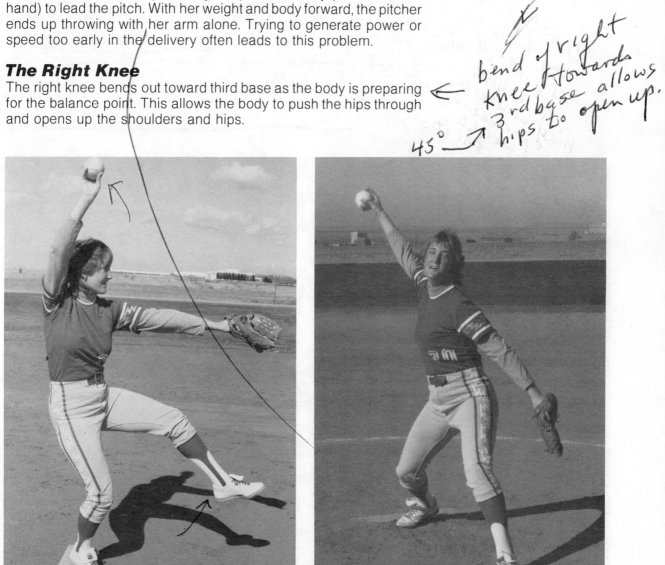

166. Position for balance point.

Easier to attain if a double-pump is used initially.

167. Right knee turned out. weight back, build momentum to power point.

Premotion

Premotion is a natural motion to prepare for the pitch. It is a controlled motion, and the body does not start the delivery or fall forward until this motion is finished. Personal preference plays a major role in the type of premotion chosen.

The Pitching Rubber

The rule states that both feet must start on contact with the pitching rubber. Most pitchers start with their right foot on top of the rubber and their left foot behind the rubber, with their toe touching the back side. Personal preference dictates the exact position because comfort is most important. It is a common fault of young pitchers to dig a hole with their right toe and then fall into that hole early in the delivery, trying to gain extra leverage to push off toward home. By coming up on her right toe early the pitcher shifts her weight forward too soon, falling on her left foot and leaving her arm to come through on its own. Her weight must be kept back until time to snap the ball.

Don't dig any holes in front of this rubber. may cause a premature weight shift.

168. Starting position on pitching rubber.

Drills

Pitchers need to spend more time in the bull pen area perfecting their delivery than on the field throwing to batters. The best way to the top of the ladder is one step at a time. Quality athletes frequently skip steps, relying on natural ability instead of correct fundamentals. To be the best pitcher possible, the athlete must master the basics first.

Fingers and Wrist Snap

- As the pitcher brings the ball through the downward swing in slow motion, the coach stands behind her and applies pressure to the ball. This resistance helps the pitcher feel the mechanics and snap. The same principle can be tested by attaching a string to the ball so that the pitcher must pull the ball through the delivery.
- Two pitchers face each other about 10 feet apart and practice snapping the ball to each other. The pitchers should use very little backswing and concentrate on cocking the ball and snapping it with a true spin to each other.
- With her forearm parallel to the ground, the pitcher cocks her wrist and practices snapping a ball straight upward, working on the wrist and spin.
- Standing with her shoulders and hips square to third base, a stride of about 4½ steps, and her arm straight above her head, the pitcher uses a slingshot motion to shift her weight back and then bring her arm forward by her body and pitch to home plate. The pitcher practices her weight shift to her back leg and the timing of the snap by her hip. Initially, the drill should be done with no hip movement, but later the pitcher should snap her hips just as the wrist snap occurs.

The Arm

- The pitcher practices arm circles as fast as possible, concentrating on feeling the complete arm extension and acceleration.
- Executing this same drill, the pitcher stands close to a fence to test whether the arm motion is in the correct plane by the body or if it wanders off to one side.

The Hips

- Using the slingshot drill described for the wrist snap, the pitcher works on the timing between the snap of her wrist and hip.

- With her feet about shoulder-width apart, the pitcher goes through her windmill motion for a distance of about 20 feet, working on cocking and snapping her hips. The pitcher can lift up on her left toe or actually pick up her left foot if she needs to.

The Left Foot

* With or without a ball, the pitcher practices taking a step with her left foot. Her step should be 4½ steps from the pitching rubber and should not cross an imaginary line drawn straight from inside her right instep toward home plate. Her toe should be pointed straight to home plate or at a 45-degree angle, but no more than that.
* The pitcher goes through her usual delivery. The coach holds a stick in front of the pitcher's left foot, forcing the pitcher to step over the stick. This teaches the pitcher the difference between stepping toward home and falling toward home.

Weight Shift and Balance Point

* The pitcher goes through her motion, stopping just as she reaches the balance point.
* The pitcher goes through her delivery, hesitating at the balance point, then finishing the pitch.

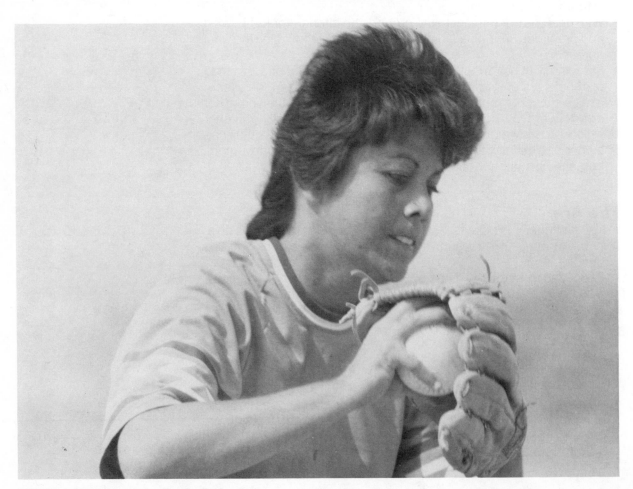

169. The pitcher must master the basics.

Flexibility and Strength

A pitcher needs flexibility, not bulk, to pitch. The arm is most effective as a whip, not a club. Any weight training should involve repetitions of light weights, with primary concentration on the fingers, wrist, forearm, and legs, not the shoulder.

Flexibility
- The pitcher takes her right hand and places it as far down the center of her back as she can, with her fingers pointing down. Her left hand pulls against her right elbow to stretch her arm muscles. Have her switch to her other hand and hold the position 30-60 seconds.
- The pitcher takes her right hand and places it back and over on her right shoulder, with her hand facing down. She places her left hand against the back of her right elbow and pushes gently against it to stretch the back or her arm. She switches arms and holds the position 30-60 seconds.
- Standing at right angles to a fence or wall, the pitcher lays her right arm against the fence, with her palm facing the fence. The pitcher then leans into the fence, stretching her arm muscles.
- The player brings her arms back behind her and parallel to the ground, with her palms facing each other. A partner gently pushes her hands closer together to stretch out her arms. Some players can stretch far enough to cross their wrists.
- With her right-hand wrist cocked back, the pitcher places the fingers of her left hand across the fingers of her right hand and stretches her fingers back toward the top of her forearm.

Strength
- The player squeezes a rubber ball.
- With a rubber band wrapped around the fingers and thumb of her right hand, the pitcher opens her hand, stretching the rubber band out. The pitcher opens and closes her hand for several repetitions.
- The coach attaches with string a light weight to a stick. The pitcher holds her arms straight out in front of her and rolls the weight up with her hands.
- In the weight room the pitcher does wrist curls with light weights.

15

Offensive Strategy

Designing an offense is like painting a picture. There are no black and white rules to fall back upon, just a coach's judgment of a situation and the infinite number of factors involved. The defensive and offensive variables are inseparable and must be dealt with as such. It is vital that the strategy reflects the available offensive talent and the opponent's defensive capabilities.

The more talented and better trained a team is, the more options there are available to a coach. Ability or the lack of it will broaden or narrow the scope of the offense. A team dominated by speed will lend itself to a running game, whereas a team with great power but little speed will require different tactics.

The heart of any offensive strategy is the execution of physical skills. Players must be well trained in the many offensive facets and be able to handle game pressures to develop a consistent attack that the coach can depend upon. For this reason, when a coach is evaluating an athlete she must know the player's talents, what she can handle mentally and emotionally, and what the player believes she can accomplish.

For example, a player may run from first to second in 3.0 seconds in practice, but be slower when attempting a steal in a game because she is being tentative. A player may be a great bunter, but in a pressure situation, such as a suicide squeeze, she may not be able to execute. The team as a whole may have good offensive potential, but lack the confidence to perform in a game. All these factors must be considered as the team goes through the season.

Not only must the offense be analyzed, but the coach must understand the opponent's defense since it will play a vital role in the total picture. Baseball and softball are the only sports where the defensive team has control of the ball. A pitcher and catcher can control a game by neutralizing the offense with good pitching and defense. A good example of this is a control pitcher who keeps the ball down consistently, which leads to many groundouts and decreases the number of long ball hits.

A coach must think out a strategy that is based on common sense and calculated on the surprise element. Avoid an offensive pattern in order to keep the defense, particularly the battery, guessing. Do not run plays on the same count, with the same number of outs, or in the same situations, because the battery will counter with pitchouts and waste pitches. The hitter should have the best pitch to hit and that extra benefit of the surprise element. At the same time, common sense must prevail. There's not much point in sacrificing a runner to second with a strong hitter when the batter on deck is weak. Nor should a coach call for a steal to second base when the hitter at the plate is weak. Plays can't be run just to run a play. There must be some purpose, some advantage gained, or there is no point in trying it.

The same can be said of lineups. There is a traditional way of setting a lineup, but a coach must also decide how best to set her offensive team in order to get the most out of the team. Many factors come into play when making up a lineup, including daily performance, physical ability, and the opponent's pitcher, but the following is a formula that can be used as a guide to making up a lineup.

First: Speed, consistent hitter, determined attitude, good base runner.

Second: Speed, good bunter, good bat control.

Third: Best hitter on the team, high batting average, good RBI hitter.

Fourth: Power, great RBI hitter, good hitting fundamentals.

Fifth: Same as fourth hitter but not as consistent a hitter.

Sixth: Good speed, contact hitter, similar to second hitter.

Seventh-Ninth: Most inconsistent hitters in lineup. If possible, look for clutch hitters or good bunters with speed.

Now that the general philosophy has been determined and the offensive and defensive teams have been analyzed, the coach must go into a game with a set plan of attack that can be revised as each situation arises. A general plan of attack is important, but a good coach must be able to make snap decisions appropriate to the existing circumstances. The following is a list of factors that must be considered.
- Opponent's strengths and weaknesses (ability, attitude).
- Pitcher (control, speed, skill).
- Catcher (alertness, arm strength).
- Defensive tendencies (alertness, backup responsibilities, plays).
- Field conditions (soft or hard infield, condition of outfield).
- Weather (sunny, cloudy, rainy, windy).
- Inning.
- Score.

- Injuries (shortstop with sore arm, defensive replacement due to injury).
- Count on hitter.
- Speed of baserunner and hitter.
- Ability of the hitter (contact hitter, bunter, power, in a slump).

Given a general plan of attack and the current situation, the coach can then structure a sensible and effective offensive strategy. A coach must always think three hitters into the lineup and be aware of which substitutes are available to help. Given certain elements, the following is an ideal situation for various offensive plays.

Hit and Run
- No outs or one out and the score is close.
- Runner at first has good speed and is a good baserunner.
- Good contact hitter at the plate, ideally left-handed.

Double Steal
- Runners at first and second with no outs or one.
- Early innings in a close game.
- Runner at second has good speed.
- Smart baserunner at first.

Delay Steal
- Any time the score is close.
- Good baserunner and slider at first.
- Second baseman, shortstop, catcher, and pitcher not paying enough attention to the runner.

Sacrifice Bunt
- No outs or one out.
- Score is even or offensive team is ahead.
- When a slow runner is at first or a run is needed.

Bunt and Run
- Good speed at first.
- Good bunter at the plate.
- Defensive team is not alert.
- No outs or one out and the score is close.

There are no shortcuts to developing an effective offensive strategy. The basics involve knowing the offensive talents of the team and being educated on the opponent's defense. From there a coach must use her own judgment and instincts to analyze ongoing situations. "Nothing ventured, nothing gained" is especially true when evaluating a team's offensive capabilities. Especially in the early season, many tactics should be tested to draw an honest picture of the offensive talents. A good coach should teach the fundamentals, know the offensive abilities, study the defense, and test the theories. Trial and error and common sense are the best teachers.

16

Defensive Strategy

Formulating a defensive strategy depends on several interrelated factors: coach's philosophy, ability of the defensive players, opponent's ability, game situation (score, inning), anticipated offensive strategy, and general conditions (weather, field conditions). This chapter first deals with the desired qualities of defensive athletes, basic positioning, and strategy. Later in this chapter, selected offensive plays are analyzed with related crucial factors that must be considered. No pat answers are provided, but rather the tools with which a defensive strategy may be built are given.

Selecting Players

Coaches would love to find nine talented athletes who are perfect softball players, but because that never happens, coaches must establish priorities and try to set their defenses around the talent that is available. When looking for infielders the coach should look for athletes who are aggressive and not afraid to field grounders. At first base a player needs a great glove to field all throws and the ability to protect against bunts and still retreat to the bag when the ball is hit. Ideally, a third baseman is strong enough to handle the hard shots and quick enough to handle bunts and the ball hit to her left. The shortstop is usually the best athlete on the team. She needs a strong arm, great range, and the ability to handle pressure situations. The second baseman should have similar qualities, but second base calls for more finesse, requiring a player who has great range and the ability to handle all kinds of throws at first in bunt plays. The qualities necessary for the pitcher and catcher are detailed later.

When choosing outfielders, a coach should look for players who can catch all types of flies, have strong arms, and are fast. If a choice has to be made, the strongest arm should be placed in right field to handle the long throw to third. The most aggressive outfielder (usually with the best speed) is chosen for center field, and the most dependable fielder is placed in left.

Positioning

First Base
- If responsible for bunts, she should play 25-30 feet from the base and 3-4 feet off the line.
- If not covering for bunts, she can play deeper, according to the ability of the hitter.

Second Base
- If first base goes in for bunts, she must play as close to first as her own talent dictates, such that she can easily sprint to first when a sacrifice or drag bunt is attempted.
- Normally shades toward second base.
- With a runner at third and less than two outs, she must play in the baseline to prevent the runner from scoring on a grounder to second.

Shortstop
- Normally shades toward second base.
- Shades toward third base if a team tends to pull the ball.
- With a runner at third, plays in the baseline to prevent the runner from scoring on a grounder.

Third Base
- If covering for a bunt, she should play 25-30 feet from the bag and 3-4 feet from the line.
- If not in a potential bunting situation, she should play deeper to cover more ground.

Center field
- Plays as close as possible and still protects against an extra-base hit.
- Shades to the left or right field alleys, depending on the hitter.

Left field
- Plays straight away and shorter against a left-handed batter.
- Plays a little shorter than left fielder.

Right field
- Plays straight away and up shorter against a right-handed batter.
- Plays a little shorter than left fielder.

General Rules

- Don't overreact when a hitter hits a foul ball. Start playing close to the lines. A hitter may be way ahead of the pitch or have hit an inside waste pitch.
- Watch the glove position of the catcher.
- Know the pitcher and her ability to control the hitters.
- Adjust to every hitter and study tendencies.
- Infielders should communicate to outfielders if a changeup is to be thrown.
- With a big lead, infielders should concentrate on getting outs, not preventing runners from scoring.
- In the late innings, players should protect the lines to prevent extra-base hits.
- Any time there is a runner at third with less than two outs, infielders should anticipate a suicide or safety squeeze.
- Fly balls that are pulled down the lines will always tail away toward foul territory.

The Pitcher's and Catcher's Role

A sophisticated strategy is based on a disciplined pitcher and catcher. If a team is to control the game, it must have a strong battery whose pitching strategy best utilizes the defensive team's strengths, thereby countering the opponent's talents and strategies. The desired game-control qualities for the pitcher and catcher follow.

170. **Sophisticated strategy is based on a disciplined pitcher and catcher.**

The catcher should:
- Control the running game with a strong, accurate arm.
- Eliminate passed balls that translate into extra bases for the offense.
- Catch all pop-ups.
- Hold on to foul tips for strikeouts.
- Handle all bunts around home plate.
- Call an intelligent game, matching the pitcher's ability to the batter and the game situation.
- Correctly block home plate and make tag plays.

The pitcher should be able to:
- Throw a desired pitch at any time.
- Throw corner strikes at any time.
- Relax and throw naturally in pressure situations.
- Field her position.

The following crucial areas are where the pitcher and catcher affect the game. Examples accompany each category.

The Pitcher's Ability

- The pitcher throws with enough speed (over 60 mph) to jam or just throw it by the hitters.
- The pitcher has a great rise that fools the hitters.

Matching the Pitcher's Ability Against the Hitter's

- Against a power-pull hitter, the pitcher uses a combination of waste pitches inside, a knuckle change, and low and away fastballs for strikes.
- Against a hitter known for her speed and bunting ability, the pitcher throws fastball pitches inside at the hands.
- Against a hard-swinging hitter who is anxious, the pitcher throws borderline strikes and off-speed pitches to try to keep the hitter off balance or make her go for a bad pitch.

Taking the Game Situation into Consideration

- With a runner at first known for her speed, the pitcher stays with speed pitches that are easy for the catcher to handle.
- With a runner or runners in scoring position, the pitcher stays with low pitches, looking for the groundout.

Anticipating Offensive Situations

- When the offensive team tends to run all its plays on a particular pitch or count, the pitcher may pitchout or waste pitches in that situation to try to second-guess the offense.
- On a count that is to the batter's advantage (e.g. 2-0, 3-1) the pitcher can pitch to the anticipated strategy. For example, if a sacrifice bunt is expected, the pitcher may throw a fastball high and inside; if a hit and run is anticipated, the strategy may be to pitch low and away, looking for a double-play ball.

Recognizing Key Players

- With runners in scoring position, the pitcher may pitch around strong hitters with intentional walks or waste pitches either to pitch to the next batter (who may be a weaker hitter) or to get the current batter to go for a bad pitch.
- With an offense that is based on speed, a pitcher may throw more fastballs or rise balls to take away the drag bunt and steals.

Adjusting to Officials

- The count is 3-2 and the best pitch to throw is high and inside, but the umpire has not called that pitch all day. The catcher needs to call a pitch that the umpire has consistently called and that stays away from the hitter's strengths.
- Regardless of the preferred strategy or even a pitcher's favorite location, a catcher must call the game that will be given to her by the umpire. If a point three inches outside the strike zone is called a strike, the catcher must use that to her advantage and not worry if a low and inside corner pitch is always called a ball.

Making Defensive Decisons

In this final section, selected offensive strategies are analyzed. A series of questions and options that must be considered by the coach before making defensive decisions are listed. There are no set answers. Each coach must evaluate the situation and come to her own conclusions. The offensive options are covered in the chapter on offense. The factors listed in the beginning of this chapter should be reviewed because they dictate the answers.

First and Third Situations

Factors
- Will the runner at first try to advance to second?
- At what point will some play be attempted?
- When will the runner at third break for home?

Options
- Allow the runner at first to advance to second with no play.
- Pretend to play the trailing runner, but actually throw the ball quickly back to the pitcher, the shortstop, or the second baseman playing in the baseline to try to catch the runner at third who is scoring.
- Fake a throw on the runner stealing second, and try to pick off the runner at third.
- Make a play on the runner going from first to second. With less than two outs expect a straight steal and throw down to the shortstop covering second. With two outs expect some kind of delay or half-way steal, and depend on a rundown to secure the out.

Sacrifice Bunts

Factors
- Does the team usually bunt with a runner at first?
- Does the team tend to bunt the ball softly or hard?
- What happens if the defense overplays the bunt? Does the hitter stay with the sacrifice, attempt a slap bunt, or hit away?
- What is the speed of the baserunner and hitter?

Options
- Play for the out at first to trade an out for advancing the runner in scoring position.
- Play for the out at second when the runner at first is slow or the bunt is too hard.
- Overplay the bunt to try to force the batter to hit away, looking for the double-play ball.

Suicide Bunts

Factors
- When is it usually attempted?
- What is the speed of the runner at third and the bunting ability of the batter?
- Where will the bunt be placed?

Options
- Guess on the play and pitchout.
- Pitch high and inside fastballs and rise balls that will be difficult to bunt.
- Pitch normally, but alert the defense to play for the bunt.

Hit and Run

Factors
- Which hitters are capable of executing the hit and run?
- In which situations is it used and how often?
- What is the speed of the batter and baserunner?

Options
- Guess on the play and pitchout.
- Keep the ball down, looking for the groundout, and pitch inside to force the hit to the left side of the infield for a better chance at a double play.
- Throw more waste pitches, hoping the hitter will be forced to hit a bad pitch.

171. The defensive players' ability will be a main factor in guiding defensive decisions.

A coach's philosophy and the defensive players' ability will be the main factors that guide all decisions. With a talented infield, a coach may meet any offensive strategy head-on, whereas a weak infield will diminish the options. The speed of the baserunner will also discourage or encourage a defensive play. Baserunners with great speed are a threat in any situation, whereas slow runners are more easily controlled. Disciplined hitters who can execute the bunt or the hit and run are a double threat and very difficult to beat.

The game situations and the anticipated offense must also be considered. In the late innings, if the defensive team is leading by more than two runs, it can concentrate on getting sure outs. In a tight ball game a team may play more conservatively and emphasize preventing the runner from scoring. Knowing the opposing coach's philosophy will reduce the surprise element and give the defense an edge on countering the offensive strategy. For instance, in a first and third situation, if a coach knows that the runner at third will not break for home until well after a throw to second base, she may try to get a quick out on the stealing runner and then look to home on the chance that a double play may catch the runner trying to score from third.

Finally, the coach and players must be aware of the weather and field conditions. A great bunting team may be hurt by a rock-hard infield. Muddy conditions will make it difficult for a running team built on speed to be effective.

The secret to designing an effective defensive strategy is taking advantage of the talents of the defensive players and knowing the capabilities of the opponent's offense. These two variables go hand in hand and, when combined with the many other factors, give the coach an advantage in any ball game.

17

Scouting Opponents

Whether coaching at the high school or college level, having a well-organized scouting system is very important. There are as many forms and methods as there are coaches, but the principles are the same.

The three types of forms described in this section are a general team scouting form, a pitch-hit statistics form, and a pitcher's form. All serve a specific purpose and, if complete, give a solid account of the opposition.

Team Scouting Form

Every coach keeps notes throughout a game in some kind of notebook. The team scouting form is a summary that can be kept as a quick reference along with detailed notes and brochures.

When studying a team's offense, hitting fundamentals, bunting, baserunning skills, strategy, tendencies, and key players should be covered. Some typical questions that should be answered in this category include the following.

- Is the team primarily a power-hitting team, or do they hit more singles backed by good team speed?
- Is the bunt used only as a sacrifice or also for a hit?
- Do the hitters try to pull the ball?
- Do the hitters seem to prefer one type of pitch (high)?
- Does the coach run an aggressive offense (hit and runs, bunt and runs) or a conservative strategy?
- Do any of the players have the speed to steal a base?
- What is the strategy in a first and third situation?
- Are there one or two key players who seem to spark the offense?
- Who does the team look to on offense?
- Who are the weak hitters or bunters?

The defensive section should detail how the team handles these same situations, but on defense, not offense. Further, any information on the ability of the players, such as strength of arms, range, and intelligence, should be noted. Obviously the pitcher and catcher will be a focal point on defense. The following questions should be answered.

- How does the infield handle bunts?
- What strategy is used in first and third situations?
- Does the team handle pressure well or tend to throw the ball away?
- Can a team steal off the catcher or other infielders?
- At what depth do the outfielders position themselves?
- Do the outfielders back up the proper infield bases in case of overthrows?
- With a runner at first, who covers third base when a sacrifice bunt is attempted?
- In stealing situations, who covers second or third base?
- Can the pitcher field her position?
- Are relays and cutoffs properly executed or can extra bases be stolen because of fundamental mistakes?

Under the heading of general comments, items such as the weather (if it affected the game), the team's attitude, and other extenuating circumstances should be noted. Later, a complete picture of all the factors that affected the game should be noted.

The pitching information should be taken directly from the pitcher's form. It should be a summary of the details on the form, but should be complete enough to describe the type of pitcher and her strengths and weaknesses. The type of information collected is detailed under the section on the pitcher's form.

Pitch-Hit Statistics Form

Every team needs some kind of hitting chart on the opposition. Some coaches write the information on charts made up of diagrams of the field to show where hits go. Some use hitting charts based on which pitch is thrown, and some just freehand the information in a notebook. In some cases, coaches take the information collected and run it through a computer for easy reference and to analyze the stats.

The best area from which to gather the information is from behind the backstop. If that is not possible, whoever is gathering the information must depend on the pitcher and catcher to help with pitch location, etc.

Whichever type of chart is selected, there should be one summary sheet that gives general information on each hitter. That sheet should describe whether she is a power or singles hitter, a bunter, a base-stealing threat, a key player, and any attitude information that will help when pitching against her. The detailed form involves deciding what information is pertinent and then designing a code and chart that fits the information onto a simple form.

One method is to follow each pitch that is thrown, define what type of pitch it was (rise, drop, fastball), where it was thrown (low and away, high and inside), whether it was a ball or strike, and what the hitter did (watched it, hit a grounder, popped up). The following is a sample key that can be used on a pitch-hit chart.

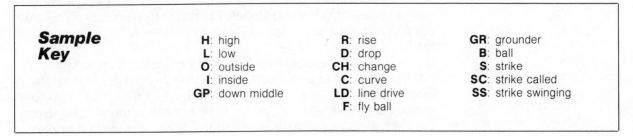

Sample Key			
	H: high	**R**: rise	**GR**: grounder
	L: low	**D**: drop	**B**: ball
	O: outside	**CH**: change	**S**: strike
	I: inside	**C**: curve	**SC**: strike called
	GP: down middle	**LD**: line drive	**SS**: strike swinging
		F: fly ball	

Circle all hits. Star any hard hits, whether an out or a hit. Take the key above and place it on a chart or a notebook, keeping track of every pitch for each hitter throughout the game. Check the following sample. The numbers indicate where the hit went.

Sample Pitch-Hit Chart	Batter	First Inning	Second Inning
	Jones	HO-B	HI-SS
		LI-SS	LO-GR-4
		GP-LD-7	
	Smith	LO-SS	
		HR-SS	
		LI-GR-6	

One sheet should be kept for each game. If a team is scouted more than once a summary sheet should be kept that can be color coded to differentiate between pitchers. The summary will show patterns. The following is a sample summary for one hitter over three games. Notice that the breakdown is based on pitch location and type of pitch.

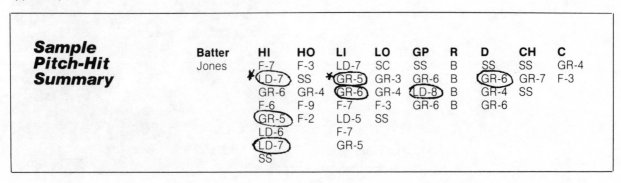

Sample Pitch-Hit Summary	Batter	HI	HO	LI	LO	GP	R	D	CH	C
	Jones	F-7	F-3	LD-7	SC	SS	B	SS	SS	GR-4
		*⃝LD-7	SS	*⃝GR-5	GR-3	GR-6	B	⃝GR-6	GR-7	F-3
		GR-6	GR-4	⃝GR-6	GR-4	⃝LD-8	B	GR-4	SS	
		F-6	F-9	F-7	F-3	GR-6	B	GR-6		
		⃝GR-5	F-2	LD-5	SS					
		LD-6		F-7						
		⃝LD-7		GR-5						
		SS								

These stats indicate that the hitter is fairly predictable. She is much stronger on inside pitches, with five of seven hits coming on inside strikes. On the other hand, she shows a tendency to pop up or hit weak flies and grounders on away pitches. She seems to lay off the rise, but tends to go for the drop ball. She does not appear to be successful with the curve or change, but there were also too few attempts to make an exact judgment.

A typical strategy against this hitter might be to waste pitches inside while hitting outside strikes. Forget the rise (except as a waste pitch or setup pitch). Hope that the hitter goes fishing for a drop or gets fooled on a change.

A color code for the various pitchers faced is important since each pitcher throws differently. Some may throw a curve that is also an off-speed drop, some rise balls move up, and some rise balls really jump. Some pitchers telegraph their pitches, others don't. Every pitcher varies in speed. Knowing the pitcher will explain apparent inconsistencies. For instance, the stats may show that a hitter pops up inside pitches from one pitcher and hits another pitcher hard on the same pitch location. The reason may be that the first pitcher throws hard and jams the hitter. If the same pattern follows a drop, it may be that one drop falls off sharply, causing the hitter to top the ball, whereas another drop may tail slowly and be hit as a low fastball.

Three games are necessary to make the stats reliable. The more games the better the stats, and the better the pitcher the truer the stats. It's also better if the games are scattered over a period of time because hitters can go through streaks, both good and bad. The most valid stats are those taken off a variety of good pitchers on a variety of weekends. All stats should be categorized and filed and kept from year to year.

172. **The more games, the better the stats.**

Pitcher's Forms

The next two types of forms are aimed at the pitcher. The first is based on the type of pitch thrown. It should show which is the most effective pitch (thrown for strikes, called or swinging, and fewest hits), which is the least effective (most hits off or thrown for balls), and which pitch or pitches the pitcher goes to when she is ahead or behind in the count. A miniature of such a chart follows.

Type of Pitch Chart

NAME _____ STYLE _____
PITCHES THROWN _____
DEFENSIVE ABILITY _____

TYPE	S	B	SO	HITS	2-0	3-1	3-2
Fastball							
Curve							
Drop							
Rise							
Change							

COMMENTS (Strength, best pitch, pattern, attitude) _____

The second type of chart focuses on pitch location, but can answer the same questions as the first chart. It will show any patterns in moving the pitch around. The patterns will be general ones (like the tendency to throw inside strikes early before setting up a strikeout with a low-away pitch), but won't show a pattern for an individual hitter. (That kind of information will be shown in the pitch-hit stats.) A smaller version of such a chart follows.

Pitch Location Chart

NAME _____ STYLE _____
PITCHES THROWN _____
DEFENSIVE ABILITY _____

SERIES	HI	MI	LI	HO	MO	LO	GP	WASTE	B
1st Pitch									
2nd Pitch									
3rd Pitch									
4th Pitch									
5th Pitch									
6th Pitch									
7th Pitch									
SPECIAL									
SO pitches									
2-0 and 3-1 pitches									

A key that depicts the type of pitch and what happens to that pitch should accompany the chart. Design the chart to hold as much information as necessary.

TEAM NAME _____ COACH _____

HITTING (power, singles, bunts, pitches preferred)_____
_____
_____

OFFENSIVE STRATEGY (sac, hit and run, bunt and run, steal, first and thirds) __
_____
_____

DEFENSIVE STRATEGY (bunt situations, first and thirds, backups)_____
_____
_____
_____

PITCHERS (name, type, strengths, weaknesses) _____
_____
_____

KEY PLAYERS_____
_____

COMMENTS_____
_____
_____

Sample General Scouting Form

Player Evaluations

Every coach goes through a variety of methods to evaluate individual players and the team's performance. Putting these evaluations in black and white facilitates the process and gives the players a clear checklist of their strengths and weaknesses while encouraging competition within the team.

The two methods detailed in this chapter serve two distinct purposes. The daily practice performance chart gives the coach up-to-date records on the day-to-day performance and attitude of each player. The game performance evaluation forms are based on a point system that pinpoints positive and negative performances during competition.

The daily practice performance chart should be kept by the head coach on a clipboard along with the daily practice schedule. It should be readily available for reference during practice. Immediately after each practice, the coach should refer to the form to add any final impressions.

Although the form has a slot for every player's name, the coach will not be able to write down elaborate comments for each individual. The form is designed to give the coach a reference that highlights each practice. Special note should be made of any outstanding plays, leadership, and attitude problems. Comments should be short and to the point. Elaborate later if necessary.

In addition to the daily log, the game performance evaluation forms provide a solid justification for starting assignments and gives players an added incentive to work for certain goals. The point system is simple, easy to understand, and a great coaching tool.

The necessary forms are shown at the end of this chapter. Players must be educated before they can fill out the forms, but either coaches or players can handle the job. Filling out the forms is good experience for the players, teaching them to identify positive and negative performances. Coaches should always supervise to make sure no points are missed in any category.

Everyone should be made aware of the purpose of each form and the intent of each category. It should be approached as a positive tool that will detail how each player contributes to the team while it provides clear individual goals. Negative points should define weak areas for a player to try to conquer.

The point system looks beyond the usual indicators to other aspects of the game that are just as important to the cause of the team, but may be overlooked by the spectacular play. A player may go zero for three at the plate, but get a walk and reach base on an error, run the bases well, score and play good defense, and compile many points. On the other hand another player may go two for three at the plate and knock in two runs, yet make mental baserunning mistakes and defensive errors that will affect her total score. Players will become aware of all the ways they can contribute to the team and take as much pride in the positive points they accumulate (or fewest number of negative points) as they usually do in their batting averages.

173. Evaluations give a clear idea of a player's strengths and weaknesses.

NAME	PERFORMANCE	ATTITUDE	*Sample Daily Performance Chart*
Player A	problem with inside pitches	working hard	
Player B	working on arcing		
Player C		good day	
Player D	blocking better		
Player E		still down from poor game—conference time	
Player F	bunting better, needs time for drag bunts	playing with confidence, positive force on team	Date _____
Player G	arm still hurt—check trainer		
Player H	angle of pursuit still poor—more grounders needed	doesn't seem to understand concepts or is lazy	
Player I	excellent day at plate	great day, lots of enthusiasm	
Player J	trying to pull ball too much—work on fence		
Player K			
Player L		working hard, good attitude	
Player M	needs work off pitchers, timing hits too much		
Player N		making excuses— needs conference	

174. The point system looks beyond the usual indicators.

Game Performance Evaluation Forms

Points for Players

Positive Points Awarded

Getting on base (except through a fielder's choice with an out involved)	5
Successful sacrifice	5
Score a run (unless a result of being on base through a fielder's choice with an out involved)	10
RBI	10
Advance a runner with no outs (other than a sacrifice)	5
Fine defensive play (catcher throwing runner out; great catch)	5
Fine defensive play that saves a run (physical or mental)	10
Alert, heads-up baserunning (coach's discretion)	5
Stolen base	5
Successful hit and run	5
Picking up signs or pitches	10
Pinch hit	5
Pinch-hit RBI	10

Negative Points Removed

Physical error that results in a run (including passed balls)	5
Each additional run that results from an error	10
Mental error that results in a run	10
Each additional run that results from an error	15
Taking a called third strike with runners in scoring position	5
Failure to advance a baserunner via a sacrifice	10
Baserunning error (overrunning a base; not running full speed; not sliding when situation calls for it)	5
Poor physical effort	10
Poor sportsmanship	5
Thrown out of a game	10
Mental error (missing signs; improper backups; getting picked off when a big lead is not needed; lack of communication between defensive players; missing cutoff)	5

Player Point System

Positive		*Negative*
	On base (except a fielder's choice)	
	Successful sacrifice	
	Advance runner a base (other than sac)	
	Fine defensive play	
	Alert, heads-up baserunning	
	Stolen base	
	Successful hit and run	
	Pinch hit	
	Score a run	
	RBI	
	Fine defensive play that saves a run	
	Picking up signs or pitches	
	Pinch RBI	
	TOTAL	
	Physical error that results in a run Each additional run	
	Mental error	
	Mental error that results in a run Each additional run	
	Take a called third strike	
	Take a called third strike with person in a scoring position	
	Failure to advance runner when called on	
	Baserunning error	
	Poor sportsmanship	
	Thrown out of game	
	TOTAL	

Game Performance Evaluation Forms, Continued.

Points for Pitchers

Positive Points Awarded

Win a game	25
Save a game	10
Groundouts (11 or more in a seven-inning game)	5
No-hitter	10
One- or two-hitter	5
Throw 91 pitches in a seven-inning game	5
Two earned runs or less in a complete game (with shutout add 5)	5
Give up two or less walks in a seven-inning game	5
Issue more than two walks but strikeout ratio is at least 2-1	5
Complete game	5

Relief Pitchers

Comes in with runners on base and does not allow a run to score, except through error	10
Faces tying or winning run without allowing it to score during the late (fifth to seventh) innings	15
Outstanding relief job (coach's discretion)	5-10

Negative Points Removed

Walk that later results in a run	5
Additional walk that results in a run that same inning	10
Walk that forces in a run	10
Walk after being ahead 0-2	10
Giving up a hit on 0-2	5
If hit on 0-2 count results in RBI or batter scoring later	10
Hitting a batter on an 0-2 count	5
Pitcher failing to properly back up a play	5
Pitcher's failure to back up results in a run scored	10
Wild pitch that results in a run	5
Each additional wild pitch in that inning	10
Crossing up catcher, resulting in runner advancing	5

Pitching Point System

Positive		*Negative*
	Win a game	
	Save a game	
	Groundouts 11 or more/7-inning game	
	No-hitter (one- or two-hitters)	
	91 pitches/7-inning game	
	One earned run/complete game	
	Shutout	
	Two or less walks	
	Issue more than 2 walks but strikeout ratio is at least 2 to 1	
	Relief pitcher comes in with men on base and does not allow a run.	
	Relief pitcher brought in to face tying or winning run without allowing to score	
	Outstanding relief job	
	TOTAL	

	Walk that results in run, additional walk that results in run same inning	
	Unsuccessful sacrifice (at least 2 strikes)	
	Hit with a pitch	
	Walk after being ahead 0-2	
	Giving up a hit on 0-2 if hit results in RBI or batter later scores.	
	Hit batter 0-2	
	Pitcher failing to back up play	
	Wild pitch that results in a run (every other run in same inning)	
	Ball that results in runners advances	
	Ball that results in runners scores	
	Crossing up catcher that advances runner(s) score	
	TOTAL	

Game Performance Evaluation Forms, Continued.

Point System Totals

Players' Names	Positive Points	Negative Points
1.	_____	_____
2.	_____	_____
3.	_____	_____
4.	_____	_____
5.	_____	_____
6.	_____	_____
7.	_____	_____
8.	_____	_____
9.	_____	_____
10.	_____	_____
11.	_____	_____
12.	_____	_____
13.	_____	_____
14.	_____	_____
15.	_____	_____
16.	_____	_____
17.	_____	_____
18.	_____	_____

Pitching Totals

	Positive Points	Negative Points
1.	_____	_____
2.	_____	_____
3.	_____	_____
4.	_____	_____

Glossary

Appeal play: A play upon which an umpire cannot make a decision until requested to by a player or coach. The appeal must be made before the next pitch, legal or illegal. An example is a base runner not tagging a base as she passes it.

Assist: A fielding credit earned by a player who helps a teammate make a putout.

Balance point: The point in the pitching delivery in which the right hand is at its highest point above the head and the left foot is at its highest point above the ground.

Backing up: A fielder moving behind a teammate to be in position to stop the ball in case of an error.

Balk: When a pitcher starts her delivery but does not immediately throw the ball to the catcher.

Baseline: A unmarked space, six feet wide, within which a runner must stay while running the bases. If the runner flagrantly moves outside this lane, she can be called out unless she is trying to avoid a fielder who is attempting to catch a batted ball.

Battery: The pitcher and catcher.

Blooper: A batted ball that flies over the infielder's head and falls in front of the outfielders for a base hit.

Beat out: When a batter hits a ball to an infielder and reaches first base before a play can be made.

Bunt: A ball tapped a short distance down either foul line or in front of home plate by a batter attempting to advance a base runner or achieve an infield hit.

Choking up: A grip in which the hitter moves her hands up the bat handle to increase bat control.

Cleanup: The fourth position in the batting order, usually given to a power hitter.

Cock: The action in which a pitcher holds the throwing hand at a right angle to the forearm in preparation for the wrist snap.

Count: The number of balls and strikes on a batter.

Covering the base: Assuming a baseman's position and responsibilities when a putout could be made at that base.

Crow hop: Using the body and arm in a throwing motion that generates maximum velocity on the ball.

Cutoff: An infielder's interception of a throw from an outfielder or another infielder when no play can be made at the intended base, or when another play is foreseen.

Delay steal: An attempt to steal a base whereby the runner does not leave until the catcher releases the ball.

Designated Hitter (DH): A hitter designated to bat for any one starting player in the game.

Do-or-die: An outfield technique used to field a ground ball on the run, enabling the outfielder to release the ball quicker and produce more force behind it.

Double play: A defensive maneuver resulting in two outs in one play.

Double steal: When two runners attempt to steal bases on the same play.

Drag bunt: When a batter executes a bunt at the last possible second in an attempt to catch the infielders by surprise, resulting in a base hit.

Drifting: Timing the flight of a fly ball with movement of the body so that both will arrive at the same point simultaneously.

Drop step: A defensive technique that allows the fielder to approach a grounder or fly in the most efficient manner and gain depth on those balls hit away from the fielder.

Earned run: A run that was scored through an offensive play rather than a defensive mistake.

Earned run average (ERA): The average number of earned runs that a pitcher allows during a full game. To determine the ERA, multiply the number of earned runs allowed by seven, then divide by total innings pitched.

Error: A misplayed ball.

Fair ball: A batted ball that is touched or stops in the field between the foul lines or that initially lands between the foul lines and beyond the bases.

Fake bunt: Assuming a bunting stance without attempting to bunt the ball. Primarily used to draw baseman in close and away from their base-covering assignments.

Fartlek: A form of training designed primarily as a conditioning modality that combines slow jogging intervals with sprint intervals.

Fielder's choice: A play in which a fielder attempts to put out one runner, allowing another runner or runners to advance safely.

Forceout: A putout on a base runner who had to advance due to the batter becoming a base runner.

Foul ball: A batted ball that is touched or stops outside the foul lines between home plate and first or third base, that bounces past first or third base in foul territory, or that first lands outside the foul lines on a fly past first or third base.

Full count: A count of three balls and two strikes on a batter.

Fungo: A self-tossed hit.

Grand-slam: A home run with a runner at each base.

Grounder: A batted ball on which no play is made before it hits or rolls on the ground.

Hit: A legally batted ball that results in a batter successfully getting on base through no error by the defense.

Hit and run: An offensive strategy in which the batter hits and the base runner steals on the pitch.

Hit batsman: A batter who is hit by a pitched ball. The batter is entitled to move to first base.

Hitting behind the runner: When a batter intentionally hits the ball to an area behind the path of a runner.

Infield fly: A fly ball hit in fair territory that can be easily caught by an infielder. With less than two outs and runners at first and second or first, second, and third, the batter is automatically out.

Interference: A hindrance by a player that prevents the defensive fielder from making a play.

Leadoff: A quick move off the base taken by a baserunner as soon as the ball leaves the pitcher's hand.

Line drive: A batted ball hit on a plane parallel to the ground.

175. Fartlek is a form of training that combines slow jogging and sprinting.

you gotta be kidding! How does this work?

jog... fart... sprint! (the sprint lasts as long as the fart)

Obstruction: An act of a fielder who, while not in possession of the ball or in the act of fielding a batted ball, impedes the progress of a base runner who is legally running bases.

Overrun: To run or slide past a base. The batter may overrun first base without being tagged out as long as the runner makes no attempt to advance to second.

Passed ball: A legally pitched ball that the catcher fails to hold and control and that the bat did not strike.

Pick off: To trap a runner off base with a sudden throw and tag for an out.

Pinch hitter: A player who is sent into a game to bat in place of another hitter.

Pinch runner: A player who is sent into a game to run for a player who has reached base.

Pitchout: A defensive tactic in which the pitcher intentionally throws a pitch wide of the plate to allow the catcher to field the ball quickly for a possible play on a baserunner.

Power point: The spot in the pitching delivery at which the perfect timing between the wrist and hip snap results in maximal force on the ball.

Premotion: A natural motion executed by a pitcher to prepare for the delivery.

Quick throw: A technique used by infielders to remove a ball from the glove as quickly as possible.

Relay: To return the ball from the outfield to the infield by using several short, quick throws rather than one long one.

Runs batted in (RBI): If a baserunner scores when a batter gets a base hit, sacrifices, forces in a run by being walked, or hits into a putout, the batter is credited with batting in a run.

Sacrifice: Advancement of a baserunner by a batter who deliberately hits the ball in such a way that the defensive fielders can only make a play on the hitter.

Shut out: To prevent the opposing team from scoring a run.

Six-twelve rotation: A top spin applied to the ball during an overhand throw.

Slingshot: A pitching delivery in which the pitcher swings the throwing arm in an arc directly back and up to a point above the head before following through by the hip and releasing the ball.

Snap throw: A throwing technique used to assure a quick and accurate throw over short distances.

Squeeze: Scoring a runner from third base to home plate by bunting the ball. The baserunner starts running as soon as the ball is pitched and the batter must bunt the ball no matter where it is pitched.

Steal: To advance to another base on the strength of baserunning alone.

Pitcher's stride: The length of the step made by the pitcher's left foot. The distance should be no more than 4½ steps of the pitcher's own foot.

Supination: Rotation of the forearm and hand so that the palm faces forward or upward.

Soft hands: When an infielder gives with the grounder by relaxing the arms, hands, and fingers as the ball enters the glove.

Tagup: The action of a baserunner touching a base while a fielder is catching a fly ball.

Trap: To catch a ball immediately after it has taken its first bounce.

Wild pitch: An inaccurately delivered pitch that the catcher has little or no chance of stopping or holding.

Windmill: A pitching delivery in which the pitcher makes a circle, starting in front of the body, swinging over the head, and ending just after the hand and arm pass the right hip.

Wrist snap: A snap of the wrist by a pitcher in order to put speed and movement on the ball.

About the Authors

**Susan Craig and
Ken Johnson.**

Coach Craig has fifteen years of ASA fastpitch playing experience and was named to several all-regional and all-conference teams during her competitive career. She has been UNM's only softball coach and was named "Coach of the Year" in the Intermountain Conference and the High Country Athletic Conference in 1981 and 1983. Susan served on the NCAA National Softball Committee and as a board member for the National Softball Coaches Association and continues to spend time working for the betterment of fastpitch softball on all levels of play.

Coach Johnson, the fundamentals coach, has 18 years of playing experience in baseball and was a shortstop on a semipro team that won two national ABCC championships. A former Lobo baseball player, he taught and coached at West Mesa High School for seven years before joining UNM's staff in 1979.